# THE LIFE HE SAVED US FOR

## Joelaan Quarles

NEW HARBOR PRESS

*RAPID CITY, SD*

Copyright © 2023 by Joelaan Quarles

All rights reserved. No part of this publication may be reproduced, distributed or transmitted in any form or by any means, including photocopying, recording, or other electronic or mechanical methods, without the prior written permission of the publisher, except in the case of brief quotations embodied in critical reviews and certain other noncommercial uses permitted by copyright law. For permission requests, write to the publisher, addressed "Attention: Permissions Coordinator," at the address below.

Quarles/New HarborPress
1601 Mt. Rushmore Rd, Ste 3288
Rapid City, SD 57701
www.newharborpress.com

Ordering Information:
Quantity sales. Special discounts are available on quantity purchases by corporations, associations, and others. For details, contact the "Special Sales Department" at the address above.

The Life He Saved Us For/Joelaan Quarles. -- 1st ed.
ISBN 978-1-63357-273-7

# Dedication

*To God . . . obviously. I mean He is the One who saved us and gave us this story. Plus, His Spirit helped me get these words all out.*

*To Devin. Thank you for believing in me and continuing to live this life with me.*

*To Enya. Thank you for saving my life so that I can share everything you taught me and tell of your legacy.*

# Dedication

# Contents

Dedication .................................................................... iii

Introduction ...................................................................1

Chapter 1: At The Scene............................................... 3

Chapter 2: Demanding The Plan .................................21

Chapter 3: Enya & God's Mercy ................................. 35

Chapter 4: Distance Between Hospital Rooms ........ 57

Chapter 5: Final ICU Days, Rehabilitation & Hopelessness ............ 67

Chapter 6: Recovery At Home ................................... 83

Chapter 7: Medications & Mental Health................. 97

Chapter 8: Sitting Still ................................................121

Chapter 9: Loneliness ................................................ 135

Chapter 10: Some Tough Questions.........................155

Chapter 11: Fear of Flying ......................................... 171

Chapter 12: Body Image .............................................195

Chapter 13: Is This Never-ending? Or Maybe It's Long-suffering .................................................217

Chapter 14: Forgiveness, Things Left Unsettled, But a Life Left to Live................................................231

Bibliography ............................................................... 243

# Introduction

IN THE FALL OF 2021, my husband, myself, and our golden pup were in a serious car accident caused by street racers. Throughout these pages I share our journey, from the scene of the crash, being transported in helicopters, our time spent in the ICU, and eventually rehab, along with our experiences throughout recovery. However, the accident is only a snippet of the story...

In the years leading up to our incident, the battle of mental health in our lives had been growing increasingly stronger, but so was our faith. Throughout our uphill climb of learning to live our lives in a new way, and attempting to adapt to our new circumstances, we have battled hardcore mental illness, loneliness, side effects, doubt, grief, and a whole lot of God in the midst of it all.

The crash has become a way to share some light from the darkest parts of our story, and my hope and prayers are that God can use the things we've learned to encourage you. Things are messy and raw, and I'm pretty good at being brutally and genuinely honest when it comes to my struggles.

So, buckle up. Maybe this is all going to make you uncomfortable, and you might grow in the opinion that I'm a nutjob at the end of all this. But don't worry... that is my opinion of myself too.

"Scars are beautiful when we see them as glorious reminders that we courageously survived."[1] - Lysa Terkeurst

"One thing I learned, is that I'm hard to kill."[2] - Molly's Game

# Chapter 1: At The Scene

*"Our life on earth is a testing ground on what kind of servant we are in heaven."* [1] *- (Anonymous)*

BASES WERE LOADED . . . or were they? Maybe just two runners were on. The concussion made things fuzzy. I was on deck, two outs, and a tie game. Friday night co-ed softball was easily one of my favorite nights of the week. Growing up in a competitive softball family my whole life, this game is where I get kick-started with Adrenaline. It was our last at bats; we just needed one run to win. The guy in front of me hit an easy base hit. *Dang it. . . I won't get to hit again.* I thought to myself. *Oh well, next week's game...*

I packed up my gear and headed for the stands to get a big hug from my hubby Devin, squeeze my doggo Enya's little face, and talk with family that had come to watch my game. After saying goodbyes to my team, our family pack started heading for our cars. We said goodbyes to Devin's parents and grandma, while my dad and his wife Jen chatted a bit with us beside our car.

Enya began to become nervous. Well, that's not the whole truth. She actually seemed quite anxious my entire game. She came every week and would walk around the fields with Devin or my dad, as she watched me play my games. This was one of our only times during the week where we weren't right beside each other. She was at my hip nearly every second of the day. In the last couple of years, she had taught herself to become my emotional support dog, but I'll talk more about this in a later chapter.

She was on edge and pulled my dad and Devin toward me the majority of the game. I thought maybe the other dogs around were making her upset (other dogs absolutely terrified her). Devin brought her over to me in the dugout each inning, but we couldn't seem to get her to relax. As we were standing by the car chatting, I remember needing to end the conversation because I thought it was best we get Enya home so she could calm down. Devin started the car, I jumped in the backseat, and Enya lay across my lap our normal car ride seating arrangements. I waved out the window to my dad and Jen, and as we backed out, I squeezed Enya tightly in my embrace, while kissing her floofy head and trying to calm her with my presence.

I didn't remember until months after, but as we were turning out of the park, my phone alerted me of a text message from my softball team's group chat. They were warning players to be careful of speeding because a police officer was nearby monitoring one of the streets. I thought about later on how convenient it would have been if the cop would have seen the street racers going by at that very moment.

***

And then I woke up ... the air seemed foggy, but with this eerie red tint. I heard Devin in the front seat—he was screaming "my leg!" I remembered not putting everything together yet; my thoughts weren't able to complete anything, but I felt a small sense of comfort knowing whatever was going on, Devin was awake and talking. I let my head fall, as my eyes couldn't see clearly. It was like looking through a telescope. I felt the weight of Enya on my lap, and though she looked out of reach through my messed-up vision, I was still trying to shake her. She wasn't moving. The stench of the airbags felt suffocating in the air, and I think at this point I started putting pieces together on what was happening. We were in an accident. I couldn't breathe; my chest felt like it was broken. I then heard, "Open the door! Open the door!" My last thought was trying to reach my arm over to the door handle so someone could help us out of the car.

*\*\*\**

I'm waking up again, but my eyes wouldn't open. I'm laying down somewhere and I hear commotion around me. I start screaming, "Devin! Devin!" I hear his voice. Still unable to open my eyes, I think I heard him near my left somewhere. I start flinging my leg toward my left, hoping I'll reach him and be able to feel him. My eyes fling open, and I see my dad and his wife by my side. I begin screaming, "Where's Enya?!" My dad points to her to the right of me, twenty to thirty feet away. I see her looking at me, but not actually at me. She must be in shock. I start yelling at my dad to not leave her alone. He's trying to sit with me and hold my hand, but I'm screaming, "Take her to the vet!" I can't stay awake.

*\*\*\**

I wake up again, and more people are around me now. Above me, I see the paramedics. They are trying to ask me something, but I'm screaming to the people around me, and my dad, to take Enya to the hospital. A woman nearby reassures me that she is going to follow my dad to the vet and take care of her. *Okay, she's going to be taken care of,* I think. The paramedics are with Devin too nearby. I still can't see him; now I'm realizing I actually can't move. But I'm yelling for Devin again, and I hear his voice. I think, *He's conscious, he's saying it's his leg.* I'm feeling thankful because in my head, he has a broken leg but no serious injuries.

The paramedics are trying to ask me something. I don't remember what, but after realizing Devin and Enya are being taken care of, I suddenly feel the brokenness in my body. I respond to them, "My chest." I didn't really think of other complaints beyond that. I became unconscious again. This is getting aggravating at this point ... it's hard to control the things around me when I can't stay awake.

\*\*\*

I wake up again. For some reason, I find it necessary to tell the paramedics not to give me narcotics. I'm not really sure why my mind went there; maybe I heard them discussing medications in my subconscious. I tell them, "Morphine is okay; I don't handle narcotics well."

I'm lying on the side of the road, with my eyes looking at the stars. I have a moment while not being able to have a full, complete thought; my body and mind somehow come to the realization ... "I might meet God soon." I feel myself going in and out of consciousness. But I start thinking about my mom. I find it so bizarre that I might see her again tonight. I begin thinking about people who have hurt me and try to formulate thoughts to make sure I'm at a good standing with those people. I don't want to pass away still holding onto hurt from others.

\*\*\*

I wake up again, and I'm in the back of an ambulance. I don't know how much time has passed, but I'm now hooked up to an IV and while the chest pain is still there, it's not as dominating. I notice my hip is hurting. There's a lot of paramedics here in the ambulance.

\*\*\*

I wake up again ... although I don't remember falling asleep. I'm on a stretcher now, being wheeled across the outfield of the softball fields I was just playing on. I feel like I'm awake, but my eyes are still dreaming. My mind is trying to put together the game: *Did we win? I don't remember what happened in our game.* I'm starting to panic a bit ... I cannot tell what is real and what my brain is making up in partial dreams in my head.

The stretcher stops, and I'm being placed into a helicopter now. With everything else around me going on, and all that has happened in the last few minutes, you'd think it wouldn't be my top concern for my fear of flying to come up. But for some reason, I find it necessary to try to voice this to one of the medics loading me in. I don't think she heard me—the propellers are so dang loud when you're right next to the helicopter.

\*\*\*

I'm wrapped up and warm; I must have fallen asleep again because I don't remember taking off, but we seem to be partway into our flight. I'm trying to say something to the girl who is sitting above my head. She can't hear me, but I reach up and grab her hand. I think she thought it was just going to be for a moment, but I had no intention of letting go. Maybe some of the shock and realization of the evening is beginning to come together. I squeeze her fingers tightly, because I am utterly terrified of flying.

\*\*\*

My eyes won't open again, but I hear the helicopter door open, and suddenly there is intense wind around me. We're on top of the hospital. My eyes open again briefly; I'm being wheeled down the long hallway.

\*\*\*

I must have fallen asleep again; I wake to people pulling at my ear piercings, trying to get them out. After all the yanking and pinching, I try to open my eyes but they aren't working again. I hear Devin nearby; we must be in the same trauma room. I begin yelling to him. The doctors around me are trying to calm me down, but I'm pretty sure I have every excuse to be flippantly flipping out right now.

They are still pulling at my piercings and aren't making any progress. I try to help but realize I can't move my left arm. I try to hold the front side of one of the piercings so they can pull off the back. This isn't working, and the pinching pain for whatever reason is bothering me more than the chest pain I'm still experiencing. I become frustrated at this point, so I start just telling them to cut the piercings off. It makes sense in my head ... I mean, they use tools to cut things out of people all the time, right?

I don't think anyone listened to my suggestions, because I wake up later and still have my piercings in. I don't hear Devin anymore ... they must have moved him to a different room to try to calm me down. My eyes are open now. A doctor comes to my side and knows my name. That's weird; I don't remember telling him my name. "Jo, you've broken your back," he begins. I don't really believe him at first, or maybe I'm just in shock. My back isn't even hurting. He then tells me I have a broken collarbone and scapula. At some point, another doctor comes over to me. I found out later he'd be my spinal surgeon. I can't keep my eyes open though ... but he's trying to show me an X-ray of my spine, I think.

I wake up to an oxygen mask on my face. Ya know, the whole point of it is to give me breath, but I feel like I'm suffocating now. I'm pulling it on and off, trying to communicate something ... maybe that I'm panicking or can't seem to breathe. But it's no use. Someone is putting it back on me, and I don't have any more energy to fight them or to stay awake.

I'm lying in the trauma room. I see the white ceiling, and out of the corners of my eyes, nurses and doctors walking around the room. I have a neck brace on and am instructed to not move my neck or back. Like I can go anywhere ... I literally can't move my body, no matter how hard I try.

\*\*\*

I didn't know I fell asleep but now I notice I don't have an oxygen mask on anymore ... thank goodness. Now I think the Adrenalin might be wearing off though. I feel panicked again. I'm trying to put together the events of the night, but the pieces are all jumbled, and my thoughts still aren't completely clear. The dreams or delusions come every time I am unconscious. I don't know what has actually happened and what is a dream anymore. I had a dream about my game—we lost though ... that's a bummer. I found out later that the dream wasn't real ... we did win the game. I also had this other dream where my big sister and her kids had called to tell me they were going to come to visit from Minnesota in a few months, and I was really excited. That I decided had to be fake because it seemed too good to be true.

Now that I'm a bit more awake, I'm begging the nurses around me to let me see Devin. One of them tells me his condition; he shattered his entire leg and would be going into emergency surgery any minute now. They say I couldn't see him. I keep asking everyone and find out Devin is asking his nurses and doctors as well.

A smiling nurse then enters the room. I haven't seen her before, but she smiles and says she has something to show me. She holds a cell phone up, and on it is a picture of my sweet pup Enya. She's in the vet ER, but she's smiling. My heart is so full of relief and tears fill my eyes. *She's going to be okay; she is alive,* I think to myself.

Finally, someone gave in, and they wheeled me out to the hallway where Devin is being wheeled into surgery. We have maybe sixty seconds together. I couldn't turn my neck, so it's hard to really see him. I'm reaching for him also, but it's nearly impossible since my left side won't move, and my right arm barely reaches across to him. We tell each other we love each other, and then he is whisked away. I'm horrified. But in that moment, I'm grateful I still don't know the extent of his injuries, or I would have been in sheer, uncontrollable panic.

I don't remember being wheeled back in the trauma room, but I'm back, and people around me are busy with who knows what medical tools. I find out Devin's family is in the waiting room, but no one is allowed in. I borrow a phone from the nurse near me to call my dad. It's a brief phone call, but I find out he is at the hospital with Enya waiting in the car. He tells me she has a concussion, but she's okay. I'm relieved to know someone is with her when I can't be, and that she's being taken care of by a team of doctors. I'm also relieved to know Devin is in surgery, and although I'm terrified, I know he is also being taken care of.

The loneliness of the moment begins to kick in. I ask to borrow the nurse's phone again so I can call my three siblings, who are out of state. I need someone here; this is the biggest thing we've ever been through. I dial the three phone numbers multiple times before realizing that all my siblings are introverts and aren't going to answer a phone call from an unknown number they don't recognize. I make a joke about it to my nurse—he must not think it's as funny as I do, because he doesn't laugh at me. I'm racking my brain for the numbers of the significant others of each of my siblings, but I can't remember any of them. I'm lucky I got the numbers right for the other phone calls I made. I give up after multiple attempts, hoping someone else is filling them in on what happened.

I fell asleep again, and when I awaken, the room is silent. I can't see any movement from my peripheral vision, and I start to get scared of being alone here. I start yelling, "Is anyone in the room with me?" but silence fills the air. I'm scared for a while, wondering why I'm not being monitored and left alone in a trauma room.

Maybe they are prepping something outside? I'm unsure but nonetheless, fear is racing through me. I can't control the circumstances around me ... I'm used to being the helper and taking care of those around me. Now my beloved dog is on the opposite side of the city and my husband is who knows where. Miles apart, and I can't help or be next to either one of them. I'm left alone with my thoughts and unsure how I'm supposed to take care of myself ... this isn't something I'm used to.

\*\*\*

I'm awake again and being wheeled into a room to get scans and an MRI of my body done. The nurse looks over my piercings in my ears and nose, determining they aren't a big deal for the imaging. I think about how I wish he would have been in the room earlier when everyone was pulling at my piercings for the immediate X-rays that needed to be done and their concerns for the piercings affecting those.

Over the next what feels like hours, although I'm sure now couldn't have been that long, I'm being prepped with earplugs, warm blankets, and soft voices trying to calm me for the scans. I assure them I've been through this kind of imaging before but still get claustrophobic every time. It takes multiple attempts to line me up properly on the bed of the scan. I start feeling a bit of pain at this point in my back, although I'm convinced now it is mostly fear triggering it after learning that my back is now broken. There's something about being lifted on and off repeatedly from a stretcher to another place by sheets after being told not to move because it could damage my spine; it's unsettling being lifted in the air honestly. I start feeling more alert at this point, but I remember asking if it is safe to take a nap while the MRI is taking place. Worried thoughts beg me to ask this question as I heard before that you can't fall asleep after having a concussion. They give me permission that it is okay, and the banging noises of the scan takes place; I drift in and out of sleep.

*\*\*\**

I don't recall the scans being finished up or being wheeled out of the imaging area. But I am now in a room that would become my ICU room for the next couple of weeks. Two nurses change me from what remained of the softball clothes that had been cut off of me at some point in the evening. I ask them about Devin and continue asking for information and updates on him the next several hours. I lay in my hospital bed afraid, exhausted, and unsure of what to do. I haven' sat still this long in ages. And I hate it.

*\*\*\**

But this was the beginning of God telling me it was time to stop. I had attempted to control and manage life in the ways that I thought were best for my family for far too long now. He kept telling me to be still and literally hold still after years of weariness and being run into the ground by exhaustion and lack of rest. There's this quote I once read in a study by Beth Moore. She said, "God will not make your life manageable; otherwise, you would manage it." [2] This was that exactly. I had absolutely no control of the events that had taken place throughout this evening, nor did I have any say in what would happen next with Devin's surgeries, Enya's injuries, or my own injuries.

This was the beginning of the end of my grip on things. I was weary and although attempting, for years on end, to hand over the reins of my anxiety and trying to hold all areas of life together, this was the end of my reign. He was taking over. And apparently the only way I would listen to Him telling me to sit still was to literally throw the brakes on in my life in the form of car brakes in a crash.

\*\*\*

I was laying in the bed, wondering when my husband would get out of surgery. Wondering if Enya was getting upset that I wasn't by her side. Wondering if I'd ever walk again. I was full of fear, but I also knew God was going to use this, even if I didn't see the whole story from beginning to end quite yet. I still couldn't remember getting hit. The last thing I recalled was reading that group text message from my team. I was trying to rack my brain, but nothing was coming to light of more details. I think I assumed it would come to mind later on after the shock wore off, but the memories still have not returned though.

The night continued on, and at some point, in the middle of the night, I was told Devin was out of surgery and sleeping in his ICU room down the hall from me. I must have assumed in my head that they would put us in the same room. But the disappointment kicked in quickly when I found that they wouldn't allow us in the same room due to Covid-19 restrictions and the extent of our injuries, leaving us in the ICU section of the hospital. I became increasingly lonelier, having my hopes dashed of getting to see Devin any time soon. I begged for visitors or for someone to get my family to come see me, but they went on to tell me visiting hours were over, and I'd have to wait until the next morning ... hours from now.

I laid in bed and every time I closed my eyes, the accident would replay over and over again ...so vividly and so real, not only in my eyes but in my body. I felt everything was still: the lack of breathing, the smell of the airbags, the weight of Enya on me, and the voice of Devin screaming. I had suffered from some childhood trauma of PTSD before in my life, mostly of flashbacks hitting me randomly throughout my adult life, and nightmares nearly every night.

But this was something different. My body was holding onto not only what I saw, but everything my senses took in and experienced in the moments after impact. I found myself trying to allow my mind to rest ... after all, there wasn't anything I could do at that moment. I would shut my eyes and be jolted awake ... again and again. Nurses came in around the clock to check vitals and monitor bloodwork, so I watched the clock for probably the entire night, counting down until I would be allowed visitors at 9 a.m.

At some point, I grabbed my bedside hospital phone and began trying to call my siblings again. I dialed and dialed, debating on leaving a voicemail, but concluding that I did not want them finding out about our accident that way. I'm not sure how many times I called, so I'll have to ask my siblings to look back at their phone calls from that evening to see how desperate I was, with the number of unknown calls they must have received.

It must have been around 4 or 5 a.m. California time at that point. After I had taken a break from trying to call for a while, I remembered there was a two-hour difference between my siblings in the Midwest, so hopefully one of them would be awake now and finally get the guts to pick up the phone from this annoying, probably scam number calling them.

The phone rang and rang as I had dialed my older sister Bry's phone. Then, it stopped ringing. But it was silent on the other end ... "Bry?" I let out. My voice was cracking; I guess it was probably sore from crying during the night. "Jo?" my heart collapsed ... I had reached her.

A little detail about me, I actually can't stand phone calls. They drive my anxiety to an all-time high and make me uneasy. But this phone call did the exact opposite. I filled my sister in on the events that had taken place in the last few hours and the results of all our injuries. She asked what I needed and who I still wanted to contact at this time . Bry took care of informing my other siblings, and people from church and other places to let them know what was going on with us. Over the next couple of hours, I was able to talk with all my siblings by phone and felt a little less alone. I told them I didn't care who, but I needed someone out here with me at the hospital.

A few hours later, I felt tired and though I was heavily medicated, the pain was not easing up. The hospital had given me all I was allowed to have of morphine, and I hesitantly agreed to allow them to treat me with a narcotic instead. I don't respond well to medication, and I never have. I will go more into detail about all this later, but something to keep in mind about me is that I'm a drug baby in a sense. My mom was heavily addicted to prescription drugs my entire life, and it wasn't until the last couple of years that we began learning more about those medications she was on while pregnant with my younger sister and me. As a result, neither of us respond well to narcotics and drugs in general.

So, the narcotics hit me like a car (maybe some pun intended there ... but hey, I can joke about it since I was the one that went through it). By the time 9 a.m. rolled around and I was allowed visitors, I remember not being able to open my eyes completely as my dad and Jen walked in my room. I felt a big weight lifted, though, when I reached for my dad's hand, unable to really speak because of being so sedated. But he was there.

It's funny to me how many times I reached for hands throughout my time in the hospital. I've talked with Devin a lot about it, and we've had many conversations about how much physical touch meant to us. We are huggers with most people, especially our families, but the idea that we reached for strangers' hands multiple times is kind of bizarre to us now. However, I feel like that is something I'll definitely carry with me throughout my life. There's something comforting about knowing someone is with us that transfers through holding a hand when we are in fearful times.

But something I've learned is that this isn't just with people who are physically next to us. God actually invites us to hold His hand as we walk through scary times. He was never absent, nor did He abandon anyone throughout the Bible. So, we can take this to heart and know with absolute certainty that He will not abandon us either. We'll talk more about this in a later chapter, about the faithfulness of God in messy, dark moments of life. But I want to share a few snippets now of quotes and Scriptures that can equip us for when we go to battle with the tragedies of this world. The way Christ worked back then in the lives and in the pages of Scripture, He works the same way now with you. He is the same God:

*"Jesus Christ is the same yesterday and today and forever"* (Heb. 13:8).

I read this quote recently in a book called *Grace for the Good Girl*:

> "Worry and fear are simply the belief that I have gotten myself into a place where God is not. And so that brings out the truth, that God, through his determination to share His heart with me, was willing to go to my ungracious place to be with me. He would rather die than live without me, even if it means ungracious places."[3] - Presten Gillham

These are some verses that back this up, which I hope encourage you if you are walking through a dark valley right now. Hold tight to these verses ... hold tight to Him:

> "The LORD your God is God; He is the faithful God, keeping his covenant of love to a thousand generations of those who love Him and keep His commands." Deuteronomy 7:9

> "Even though I walk through the darkest valley, I will fear no evil, for you are with me, your rod and your staff, they comfort me. You prepare a table before me in the presence of my enemies. You anoint my head with oil; my cup overflows. Surely your goodness and love will follow me all the days of my life, and I will dwell in the house of the Lord forever." Psalm 23:4-6

> "Suddenly, a furious storm came up on the lake, so that the waves swept over the boat. But Jesus was sleeping. The disciples went and woke him, saying, "Lord, save us! We're going to drown!" He replied, "You of little faith, why are you so afraid?" Then he got up and rebuked the winds

*and the waves, and it was completely calm. The men were amazed and asked, "What kind of a man is this? Even the winds and the waves obey him!" Matthew 8:24-27*

I'm wrapping up this chapter for now, but a few final thoughts on that last verse from Matthew 8 that kind of hit home for me, so I think they need to be acknowledged. First thing ... the verse starts out with "Suddenly." Although Matthew is writing this from his personal experience, the event of the storm on the lake seems to him like it came out of left field, seemingly all of a sudden in his life. I think it's important to remember that we think like this too ... well, at least I do.

There have been multiple occasions where something tragic or scary happens out of the blue and starts throwing off my groove in life. But it's only sudden to me; it was never sudden or unknown to God. And I think we can find some comfort in that, knowing that He sees all, knows all, and is with all through all that has and will happen, as we climb the mountains and walk through the valleys of this life.

The second thing that draws my attention is there is the line in this passage that talks about how the disciples went to Jesus and were basically freaking out with the storm hitting them. They were terrified of drowning, as one of them puts it. But it makes me wonder which one of them actually said the words, "Lord, save us! We are going to drown!" Sure, maybe that was just the gist of what multiple people were yelling to Jesus about, but I highly doubt all of them were in unison saying the exact same words in their fear. I can't know for sure, since I wasn't there, but I do wonder which disciple was freaking out so much that he thought it necessary to tell these words to Christ.

I don't want to be like that every time something gets chaotic. I know God wants us to come to Him in our fear, but I also don't want to forget that a big part of our faith means putting our trust in Him into practice. I want to be a disciple of Him, and even in the midst of fearful circumstances, to be able to have faith that He isn't ignoring my fears or the scary situation around me. He's there with me. The only difference is that He isn't scared. I never want to have an outburst of fear. I want to approach Him in my prayers and bring my fear to Him, knowing full well that He already knows the situation. The only point in talking to Him about it is not to make Him aware, but to make my heart and my circumstances aware of Him.

*"Worry is something you create."*
*"Why would we create worry?"*
*"To fill a void."*
*"A void of what?"*
*"Faith."*[4]

- Mitch Albom; *Stranger in the lifeboat*

# Chapter 2: Demanding The Plan

*"We were never meant to bear the weight of having it all figured out. But we are meant to trust the One who does."*
[1] *-Kaley Olson*

Devin and I would go on to spend the next two weeks in our separate ICU rooms in the hospital. The first couple of days were full of a lot of heartache, confusion, fear, others trying to help us fill in the gaps on the night before and the events that took place, and a whole lot of questions as to why this was all happening. I'm pretty sure I asked nearly every person who came to visit me the same exact question. I'd say, "I know God is going to use this, even if I can never walk again, but what is this all for?"

It sounds a bit silly when I write this out. I look back now, and the idea of trying to demand the plan to be all laid out for me is not relying on God or trusting Him through it all. In my head, I kept telling myself that I was in the right mindset to ask this kind of question. I trusted that Christ would indeed use it someday, and I wasn't mad at Him in any sense for the circumstances we were facing. I think I was just eager to understand how He was going to use it so that I could find some hope in it right then and there. I believed in my mind that if I saw that hope and could grasp onto His end plan, it would give me endurance and perseverance to look forward to the result.

But as I write this now, and look upon these words, I discovered that I really wasn't trusting God at all. I think of it like this: Devin and I enjoy being out in nature, hiking beautiful mountains, trails, and fields that our Creator has so perfectly made. However, when we're looking into our next adventure, I usually try to peek at an online photo to see the end view of the journey. Oftentimes if it's not something super majestic, or Instagram photo-worthy if you will, I will usually skip it, and we'll find something that feels more worth the climb. I have absolutely no issue hiking twenty miles if it means seeing something cool at the end of it.

And the funny thing is that life kind of goes the same way in my mind. I can accept the hard challenges, the difficult confrontations with others, the scary diagnoses, and the "no" to the things I want so desperately. I tell God, "Yeah, I trust you! You're going to use this for something cool, and to grow me through it!" But when I'm in the middle of the path that's uneven, where there's no wildflowers, pretty sunsets, or waterfalls, that's where I get discouraged.

The reality of it all is that I can say all day long that I trust Him. But it is not real faith or trust in Him unless I'm willing to walk through the dark fields of life, not knowing what He has allowed around the corner. So, when it came to laying in the hospital bed ... Yes, I believed with all my heart that He had a purpose, but I wasn't willing to walk through the valley without demanding a glimpse of the mountaintop first.

This is a pattern I still struggle with, even today as I write about how messed up it is. I'm working on it, trust me, but I share because I don't believe I'm the only one in the world who battles this. So, I want to help with some of the things I've learned along the way, hopefully encouraging you but also calling you out as a fellow Christ follower. We try to take the reins on things in life when we aren't getting answers—when it seems like it is taking too long, and the journey is too slow while we're aiming for that Insta-perfect view. We try to run ahead to catch it before we were intended to reach it.

I'll be honest in saying that I still have absolutely no idea why we were in such a terrible accident. I don't know if I'll ever be able to lift my sweet nieces and nephews in my arms again, as they exceed my 20-lb. lifting restriction. I don't know if Devin's leg will fully recover, and if his limp will go away. I don't know why our sweet Enya was taken when she had so much excitement for the life she could have continued to live. And in reality, I may never get those questions answered. But I've been learning through this seemingly endless recovery process that it isn't, and never was, about seeing God's end-goal plan. He's probably tried to tell me a million times in that hospital bed, and I talked over Him instead, demanding His plan. It's that old cheesy saying: "It's about the journey, not the destination."

Now I say this all while still knowing that, realistically, it's hard to just let go and sit along for the ride when disaster has struck. I understand that you have gone through, or are currently walking, in a time of uncertainty, but it requires action. God asks us to trust Him by hanging on when the waves get super chaotic and bumpy. But we don't just grab His hand and then plop our butts down to scroll through social media, distract ourselves with Netflix, or seek things that will numb our minds and hearts to the pain around us.

No, we are called to trust Him by not trying to control the wheel of our spinning world, but instead to seek the paths ahead He has set in front of us so that we can take action. For me, in the hospital, that looked like asking tough questions. I wasn't sure if Devin, myself, or Enya would ever walk again. An option available to me would have been ignoring those realities, or even turning to God and becoming angry with these new circumstances. I could have flipped out and become anxiously overwhelmed with all the surgeries, treatments, and therapies that were to come. But neither of those were going to help me get to the mountaintop any quicker. The valley was where I was at, so I needed to ask the Guide in front of me questions as He led me forward. He was the only One who knew the path, where the holes were, where the sharp rocks I needed to step over and avoid were located, and where the waters were that I would need to grab His hand in order to walk through.

In a therapy session, I once learned that it isn't a matter of dropping everything; it's where we place it. We drop things in a holy way when we don't just drop them without care in the dirt, but instead we intentionally let go by placing them in the safety of God's hands. Releasing our grip on things should never be an act of carelessness; rather, it needs to be an intentional act of surrender to Christ.

When we release them, we are saying to Him, with confidence, "I trust you to keep these things that I hold so close to my heart safe." Here are some verses in the Bible that are helping with convicting and encouraging me to let go of my grip on things that I want to control in my life.

*"Cast all your anxiety on Him because He cares for you." 1 Peter 5:7*

*"Do not be anxious about anything, but in every situation, by prayer and petition, with thanksgiving, present your requests to God."* Philippians 4:6

*"And we know that in all things God works for the good of those who love him, who have been called according to his purpose."* Romans 8:28

*"You keep him in perfect peace whose mind is stayed on you, because he trusts in you."* Isaiah 26:3

*"Commit your way to the LORD; trust in Him, and he will act."* Psalm 37:5

*"And without faith it is impossible to please him, for whoever would draw near to God must believe that He exists and that he rewards those who seek Him."* Hebrews 11:6

*"In all your ways acknowledge him, and he will make straight your paths."* Proverbs 3:6

*"We have this hope as an anchor for the soul, firm and secure."* Hebrews 6:19

I like the idea that we can have an anchor of hope in Him. An anchor holds steadily, making sure the boat attached to it doesn't get swept away. Letting go and letting God does not mean letting everything in life go frantic and come loose or undone. Letting go requires handing ropes over to someone else (Jesus). It requires us to trust where we throw our anchors down.

If you Google the definition of the word *secure*, it's described as "being fixed or fastened so as not to give way, become loose, or be lost. 'Check to ensure that all nuts and bolts are secure,' tight, firm, fixed." [2] I love that ... "firm and secure." Just like how it's written in Hebrews 6:19.

So, it leads me to these questions for you:

- Where are you placing your anchor when life is pulling you into the rocky waves?
- Are you setting it in the sand, or, in realistic terms, in the hopes of things that aren't of Christ? Things that are ever-changing, according to the flow of the tides surrounding it?
- Or are you handing the ropes over to the firm hands of our Father?

I encourage you today: release your grip that is burning up your hands and hand over the anchor to the One who can fasten it securely and firmly in place.

*****

### God's will VS Satan's plan

"This is the will of God; don't worry."
"Satan is just trying to mess with God's plan for you."
"God won't give you anything that you can't handle."

False. Every single one of these lines. These are just a handful of some of the "comforting" words we were told throughout our journey. I remember thinking along the way how I don't believe that hurting His children is a part of God's will. I also don't believe the devil was out to get us or able to mess with God's plan. So, I'll say this: we aren't in God's "will" or "plan" in the middle of disasters. Now before you tune me out, hang out just a second and keep reading.

The Bible is very clear that the Lord is everywhere, knows everything, and sees all that is to come.

*"Great is our Lord, abundant in power; his understanding is beyond measure." Psalm 147:5*

*"Your eyes saw my unformed substance; in your book were written, every one of them, the days that were formed for me, when as yet there was none of them." Psalm 139:16*

*"I am the Alpha and the Omega," says the Lord God, "who is and who was and who is to come, the Almighty." Revelation 1:8*

*"These things God has revealed to us through the Spirit. For the Spirit searches everything, even the depths of God." 1 Corinthians 2:10*

*"For my thoughts are not your thoughts, neither are your ways my ways, declares the LORD. For as the heavens are higher than the earth, so are my ways higher than your ways and my thoughts than your thoughts." Isaiah 55:8-9*

I want you to take note that I didn't add the verse Jeremiah 29:11 in order to drive home the idea about God's will. Often, the verse from Jeremiah is taken out of context and people claim that promise when it was never intended for them. We can learn from it, yes; from it, we see that the same God who was working during that time is still our same God today. He is able to perform and restore us out of brokenness. But He does not promise to save us from every difficult thing in our life. He still allows pain, hardships, and even death to happen because we live in a fallen world. BUT just because He allows it does not mean that it is His will.

I was talking with Devin about this topic earlier this week, and we were discussing this whole concept of bad things happening in life, and the presence of God and Satan in the midst of it. He brought up this point that really got me thinking and stretched my thoughts, explaining it this way: "I believe that Satan has given more people the winning lottery ticket vs. the amount of people he has killed."

If that sounds confusing right off the bat, let me dig a little deeper. Let's look at our car accident. Do I believe it was an evil scheme from Satan? That he just had to throw that in our lives because we were too close to messing up his intentions and getting too close to God? Actually, I really don't believe that. So, you might think, *Oh, okay, so you think this was God's will for you guys?* Nope again. I don't think Christ was sitting on His throne and decided that those guys racing needed to crash into us in order to complete His plan for us as His children. But I do think that He allowed it. I know He foresaw it, and I believe with everything that He is going to use it, whether in this life or in eternity.

Though, at the same time, I don't think for a second that Christ has enjoyed watching what we have been through. I don't think He was smiling when we were laying on the side of the road. I don't think He was thinking about something else or just going about His day while we were going through life-threatening surgeries. I believe His heart was aching, His eyes probably watering, and His mind thinking about how He wished it didn't have to be this way, all the while allowing it to take place.

First Peter 4:19 says this, *"Therefore let those who suffer according to God's will entrust their souls to a faithful Creator while doing good."* Again, I don't believe it's God wanting us to suffer. He allows the suffering to happen in order to grow us into His good and perfect, purposeful will.

You might argue that it was then Satan's intentions to hurt us and bring us down. Maybe, but honestly, if Satan wants to bring us closer to him, wouldn't he continue in his pattern of deceit that he is so well known for? Wouldn't he continue in the ways that he has pulled others from Christ for centuries, by giving them exactly what they want in life? I've heard it said before that the devil doesn't walk around with horns and a pitchfork. No, instead he walks around in front of us clothed in our deepest desires.

One of the most dangerous things I believe the devil does to attack followers of Christ is to give them everything they want. I've seen far more people fall away from God by being successful in their jobs, getting their dream homes, the perfect significant others, and the like. But the scarier thing in all of this is that a lot of people don't even realize they've fallen away from Him. They have gone on running after and living in their success, all while thinking they are experiencing the blessings God has given them. Side note, yes, all our blessings are from Him, BUT just because our blessings are overflowing does not mean we are in right standing or following the will of Christ.

In my life, I've never gone through a suffering moment and felt the urge to run to Satan. In those moments of deep heartache, confusion, and pain, I run to the Father and crave His embrace of peace and safety. So, if at the end of this book, you still think that this was on the devil and his plan was to put us through this accident, then I can tell you that he messed up, because it didn't work. Not for a second.

*****

The first morning in the ICU was extremely stressful. Not only was it a time of trying to accept our new circumstances, but the constant testing and monitoring going on was unbelievable. I didn't know you could be poked so many times for blood tests and need so much supervision on the results of those tests. Devin and I both lost a lot of blood, and the result of that was our bodies went into panic, and our normal blood pressure and blood levels were all out of whack.

I'm incredibly thankful that neither Devin nor myself realized the extent of his injuries during the accident. God has one hundred percent guarded our minds from the trauma that we went through. We found out later on, before the accident occurred, that we were nearly stopped and approaching a red light when the street racer lost control and swerved into our lane, hitting driver to driver. Due to being in a manual car, Devin was holding his leg down on the clutch at the moment of impact. His entire leg was shattered. His femur went through his skin, and he was bleeding out. We were told later by another doctor working in the emergency room that night that he was in charge of holding Devin's ankle as they stabilized him, because his ankle was essentially falling off. Terrifying, right? We have Christ to thank for the protection of shock that He placed on our minds. We don't have to look back at those memories today because of Him.

Due to all these major injuries to Devin's body, and my broken bones, we were given more vitamins and medications than I could keep track of each day. Devin's blood pressure was through the roof, and mine was dropping dangerously low. I became anemic due to extremely low iron levels; I also lacked calcium and vitamin C, and a handful of other issues that affected my blood stream. We both came extremely close to needing blood transfusions, which terrified us.

We each had a different doctor for each broken bone we experienced: we also had doctors that focused on our medications, doctors that focused on our rehabilitation, and doctors for every other area of help we needed. And that's not even including all the nurses we had coming in and out of our rooms! It was a lot of social interaction for the introvert writing this, let me tell you. But the weird thing is I struggle a bit with remembering certain times of those two weeks. I'm sure a big part of it was the medications and being in shock for a good portion of it as well.

However, there is an interaction that really sticks out to me and kind of gnaws at me to this day. I said in the first chapter that I had my first interaction with my spinal surgeon the night I was brought into the ER. That moment is a bit fuzzy in my mind, but I distinctly remember the second interaction with him. He came into my room Saturday, late in the morning, and the words he said to me will be ingrained in my mind unfortunately for a long time, if not my whole life. We were discussing how I was feeling, and he responded to me with these words: "Well, you can be happy knowing that the guy that hit you died."

Ouch ... umm, that most definitely did not make me happy. My heart felt crushed, and sickness in my stomach arose. I wasn't angry with the man that hit us. Sure, I was really upset with the entire situation, but wishing death upon someone? That I just cannot understand. I'll go more into our lessons that we've learned on forgiveness in a different chapter. But I will say I've struggled with the idea of knowing that someone who works at a job saving other people's lives was okay with the idea that someone passed away.

It's not my place to pass judgment; however, it's not the only time I encountered words that related to that kind of mentality. I heard so many people call the driver that hit us stupid and dumb. And while he made a dumb decision, I don't believe he was stupid. This was another human being that God created, whose poor decision unfortunately cost him his life. I think about him often and wonder if he believed in God. And I really hope he did, because he didn't have a chance to regret the mistake he made that evening.

I know a lot of people out there are mad and upset for us at the two racers, but that's not really what we need. At the end of it all, we need people to make changes. If you are angry that someone made this decision while driving, then be the one to change and drive smarter in your own car.

I've been in different cars with a wide range of people since our accident, most of whom are angry at the drag racers. But at the same time, a lot of those who are angry about this situation still continue to speed, still continue to text and drive, still continue to not wear a seat-belt. If you're angry about what happened to us, why do you participate in similar acts? This may seem like a weird topic for a book, but I've also become very passionate in this area and respectful to the rules and authorities that have been put in place while we are on the road.

The rules are there to protect us, not to ruin our fun time or put a downer on the drive. In the same way that Christ has set rules and boundaries in His Word, we also have rules and boundaries to protect us in everyday life as well. God tells us not to have sex before marriage, not to become drunk to the point of being unsober in our minds, not to murder, not to steal, etc. You think God wants to ruin your happiness and not support sleeping together before your wedding night? It's not to ruin it it's to protect it. It's for YOU to guard your heart and mind and give you the gift of this amazing joy to share with one person on the special night He has planned.

Do you think He wants to be a buzzkill (okay, might have had some pun intended there) and tell you to be careful not to become drunk? It's for your safety. It's so you can be alert and safe, so that you don't endanger yourself or someone else. It's so you can learn to be reliant on and filled with His Spirit, not from the spirits of this world. The same goes for murder and stealing. These aren't to hold someone back—they are to protect His kids from harm.

So, I just want to close on this. If you think the rules on the road are dumb, that sucks, but they are still there for you and others. If you are angry with us, then be angry in a way to encourage others and drive home the point of protecting yourself and others to the best of your ability while in a motorized vehicle. If you want to get angry at the people enforcing these rules or blame them when they catch you not listening to them, please check your heart. They are living vessels that God has put in the place of authority to watch over His kids and, in this case, His kids playing in the street.

*"For lack of guidance a nation falls, but victor is won through many advisers." Proverbs 11:14*

*"Everyone must submit himself to the governing authorities, for there is no authority except that which God has established. The authorities that exist have been established by God."*

*Romans 13:1*

# Chapter 3: Enya & God's Mercy

*"Her absence is like the sky, spread over everything."* [1]
-C.S. Lewis

I'M NOT REALLY SURE how to do this. How do you capture the description of someone God put in your life who was there during it all? How do you tell the legacy of someone who you love so much? How do you tell the story of the one who shielded your life with hers? Honestly, this chapter is going to be severely tough. I'm dreading writing this chapter because I know my eyes will be blurry with tears as I stare at this screen, typing these words. But at the same time, I'm so eager to share this story with others. This is the legacy of Enya Shanessa O'shea, the pup who gave her life for mine. I want to honor her with all that I am.

When I tell someone that I lost my dog, nine times out of ten, I get the same sad face and "I'm sorry" response. But I also see the confusion as to why I'm so torn up about someone that wasn't human. I think it might help to understand that Enya was not the first dog I've lost. In fact, my family raised Enya's entire family growing up, and it hurts my heart to say that we lost each of them as well. I held the paws and squeezed them in an embrace as they took their final breaths. I watched as they battled tough medical diagnoses and sat in many waiting rooms of vet offices while tests and treatments were performed. I was once broken and unsure how to carry on when we had to say goodbye to my best friends as their hearts beat one last time.

    I faced similar confusion in others during those losses as well. I remember growing up and being there when my friends would lose a pet; they seemed to handle it a lot better than me. I have memories of friends laughing and wanting to hang out and forget the whole thing that very same day of their loss. But me—I went into deep sadness and sorrow. Weeks would go by where I wouldn't want to talk to anyone or go outside and leave the house. When I look back now, I realize I hung on to my dogs very tightly because they were never just animals to me. They were my best friends, like siblings oftentimes, and they understood the everyday life that took place within the walls of our home.

    My home growing up was not a safe place. There was deep hurt and pain caused from emotional and physical abuse. I grew up being terrified of a mom who would often make those in the house walk on eggshells, with everyone just bracing for the next explosion to occur. And there's something about having my pups around that brought elements of safety in those dark times that I didn't have from anyone else. Maybe you'll disagree with me, but I know God had my dogs purposefully placed in our home to show a sense of protection and comfort in scary times. Sheamus, who was Enya's dad, was our very first Golden Retriever pup. He offered a sense of unconditional patience and had no anger in his whole being. He was the one you'd step on by accident, and he would look up at you with his big brown eyes and look like he was trying to apologize to you. He'd lick your tears if you were crying and show the opposite of the chaos that was all around our home he was the calmness in the storm.

Shanae was Enya's mama; we got her the week of my eighth birthday. I'll always remember my family telling me we had to go pay an important bill, only to show up on a huge property and be surrounded by multiple families of Golden Retrievers. We took her home, and she was a bullet that I know shocked Sheamus beyond belief. They were total opposites but became incredibly close and loved each other so well. The funny thing with Shanae is that I think the intention was that she'd be closest with me. But ya know the interesting part of it is that Shanae, or Nanny as we always called her, became insanely close with my mom. It was really bizarre in my mind, because I'd watch Nanny when my mom would be in big rages. She would sometimes hide under the table, maybe scared of getting hit by something my mom was throwing. But other times, she would run up to my mom and bury her head in my mom's lap. She would nudge her consistently, and often this would settle my mom for a few moments. Nanny was a picture of unconditional love, despite how others may act around you.

In 2006, Nanny and Sheamus had their litter of six puppies and 1 angel pup (who passed on). We were overjoyed, and my little ten-year-old self had trouble wrapping my mind around it all with the overwhelming cuteness and love of his furry family. From the litter, we kept the only boy, who we named Moose Mcgillicuddy. This name was brought on due to his giant head and his towering body over his sisters. The second pup we kept was the darkest, and the only little redhead of the bunch. She matched her daddy, and though she was tiny, she was mighty and made herself known from the get-go. This was the beginning of Enya's story.

I have distinct memories of Enya being in her little gated pen with her siblings and mama as they slept in the middle of our living room. Enya would howl and almost scream most nights until someone would run in and pick her up to hold her. She wanted all eyes on her and the embrace of someone holding her at all moments. She wouldn't sleep or relax without someone running in to be with her. This stubborn spirit is something that continued on every day of her life.

Enya and Gilly (Moose's nickname) stayed with us, but the others ended up going to friends and staying nearby; it was incredibly hard having to part with them. I'm pretty sure I begged to keep them all every time we had to start saying goodbye. Teagaan, Failta, Brynne, Brenna, and our angel pup Rookie: these pups brought my heart joy and comfort throughout that summer that I will never forget. Those first few months were spent outside chasing puppies and getting into trouble, playing with piles of ice cubes to stay cool that acted as chew toys to little puppy teeth wanting to nibble on everything. That summer I will hold in my heart forever.

As time went on, our new normal in our household consisted of four Golden Retrievers running the house. In fact, the rule in our home was that "you never make a dog move," and they definitely took advantage of this. Oftentimes, even nowadays, it's my norm to go grab a seat on the floor instead of furniture. I think this comes from years of taking a seat on the floor nearby the four Goldens sprawled out comfortably on our couches.

It took the whole family to walk them all, and I'm sure the neighbors thought we were insane as we herded our giant parade of six humans and four giant dogs down the street most days. Our pups slept snuggled up next to someone always in our beds, put up with being dressed up by us for tea parties or just on a normal Tuesday. They showed patience and love, and even though I'm pretty sure I saw them roll their eyes at us on multiple occasions, they continued to bring love and laughter in the brokenness our home often carried.

There was always a furry paw to hold when times got tough. There was a furry chest always ready to soak up tears. There were slobbery tongues waiting to lick the snot away from our dripping noses. They were there, even scared like us ... but I knew they were a tangible hope to grab onto when I felt stuck and in a dark pit. They constantly found ways to make us laugh, even on the hardest nights: whether it was from Sheamus howling in his dreams, or when he would refuse to eat dog food so we'd be forced to go get him McDonald's burgers so that he wouldn't go to bed hungry. Or Nanny running like the Tasmanian Devil around the house, trying to get someone to chase her; or her bark that sounded exactly like a rooster whenever she got going.

Then there was Gilly, who would drag every single stuffed animal out of our bedrooms and walk into the living room with the biggest smile and the wiggliest butt (we called this his happy butt). He would always get picked on by the girl pups, and they would team up against him when they'd have their daily wrestling sessions. Gilly, like his dad, showed complete patience and was slow to anger. He had the gift of klutziness and knocked down everything in his path without even noticing.

Often, he would sleep in my bed, or, let me rephrase that; he would lay on my bedroom floor moaning until I gave him an invite to come up on the bed. And then when I did, he wouldn't sleep next to me. No, this 70-lb. dog would need to lay on top of my body. He showed me unconditional cuddles and warmth, even on the hardest days.

And then there was Enya, who was a mini version of her mommy. Her energy seemed unending, always running around. She was always getting into mischief, whether by running around the yard chasing Gilly, or coming up with the plan to eat two batches of chocolate cupcakes we had cooling one Christmas on the counter. Somehow, she demolished the plan to do this while we opened presents, and so quietly that we didn't even notice until she was nearly finished with them all. Side note, she never even got sick from all that chocolate!! Enya showed the gift of stubbornness and unconditional joy, even in the midst of all kinds of trouble.

And then there was the period of time after my grandma passed away when I was a freshman in high school. Her Pomeranian Tiki hated just about everyone except for her, and then when she passed, he clung to me. It was less than a year that he joined our clan and bossed all the giant dogs above him around. He kept them in line by running the show, and they were terrified to talk back to him. Just nine months after we lost my grandma, Tiki suddenly began acting weird overnight. Early the next morning, we took him to the vet, thinking he was just not feeling good. After being taken back to get testing done, the vet ran back out with him in her arms to us. She set him in my arms and explained he was having a heart attack. I held him as he had his last moments on earth. However, I don't believe he passed from a heart attack; I believe his heart was broken because he missed my grandma so much. "A dog is the only thing on earth that loves you more than he loves himself." [2]-Josh Billings. I think his purpose was to be there and to love my grandma, and he absolutely fulfilled that purpose.

So now that you have a little snippet of the backstory behind my family of pups, I hope you grasp even a tiny bit of the protection and love that they provided. When Sheamus passed away at thirteen from continual seizures and undiagnosed brain issues, a chunk of my safety and love that I got to give to and receive from was ripped away. Just seven months later, Nanny's lymphoma became increasingly aggressive, and treatments stopped working. Just a few weeks before she would have turned nine years old, Shanae passed away; another safety net and loving support was gone.

That next year was extremely difficult, not just on us but the depression that we watched their babies Enya and Gilly go through from losing their parents. It was utterly heartbreaking. I could see the fear not only in my own life, but in the eyes of their pups. We felt together like we were picking up pieces and living in a new fear of uncertainty. Gilly and Enya had new roles to play, and they showed so much strength as I watched them rise from the ashes of terrible pain and continue on to love and protect my family and me, despite so much loss.

They loved us well. They were the place I'd run to when I needed comfort or to vent about a tough day. They brought joy and laughter throughout those years, despite the abuse around us, despite the diagnoses, the family we lost, the heartache that all went on. Whenever I walked in the door, no matter how terrible I was feeling, Enya and Gilly would fill my heart with joy every single day.

In the beginning of 2020, Gilly started growing weaker after continually not being able to eat after weeks of medications and

X-rays and all kinds of testing. I swore to never put a pup to sleep in my life. In my mind, that meant giving up hope on a miracle and, in a way, trying to play God with making this kind of decision. But Gilly's pain was growing worse, and his moaning and lack of being able to stand now was too much. I couldn't allow him to suffer any longer. I will always remember that morning; I told my dad it was time to make the call, as Gilly didn't need to hurt anymore. For thirteen years, he protected me from pain, and now it was my turn to try to do the same for him.

I remember feeling so incredibly guilty and scared as Enya lay nearby where Devin and I had been laying on the ground, holding Gilly each night. We were wrapped in blankets, and Enya was sound asleep at Gilly's and my feet. I was so scared of hurting her, of causing her pain and the heartbreak that was coming with having to say goodbye to her brother. I feared she would be upset with me. That she would hurt because of me.

When the vet walked in the door, Enya didn't bark. This was unusual; she literally barked at everything and everyone. In fact, she seemed calmer than I think I had ever seen her. She seemed to know who his woman was, and there was something in Enya's eyes that showed she knew this was necessary to take her brother's pain away. Enya sat close by; I held Gilly tightly wrapped in my arms as we said goodbye.

That afternoon, I was terrified. I went from wanting to live in my endless hole of grief to realizing that Enya was at risk for becoming depressed again since Gilly was gone. Something I didn't mention before is that our dogs loved each other but were absolutely awful at socializing. I recall a handful of times we attempted to take them all to the park together to run around and hopefully meet new friends. But each time, it would queue a panic attack not just in my life but in every member of our family. My mom held this anxiety that was passed down to us surrounding her. Each time the dogs would get off their leashes, I went into a full-blown panic attack of them running away, running into the street, or getting hurt. I wanted to hold on tightly because I couldn't lose them.

Each park attempt would turn into a blowup at our house later on. Everyone was on edge, and in a panic from the afternoon festivities. So, after a few attempts, the efforts were dropped and dog walks in the neighborhood were the norm. I felt bad at the time. Our dogs were seemingly being isolated more than other dogs I knew that were out and getting to socialize. But our pups actually didn't seem to mind. They had us, and they seemed to love the time they got to just spend in our home and yard without needing other pups from the outside world.

So, when we lost Gilly, my first thought was *I'm not going to let Enya become lonely.* We loaded her up in our Mini Cooper for a car ride (which she usually hated). Car rides meant one thing throughout the years it's time for the vet. So, when we pulled in just a few minutes later to a nearby park, Enya seemed confused and out of her mind. She didn't know how to act or what to do in the big, open field of green in front of her. I think we may have lasted five minutes before she was begging to get back in the car again.

With that being a bust on cheering her up, we went through the McDonald's drive-thru and got her an ice cream cone. Confused at first, but a few minutes later understanding what a treat this was, this seemed to do the trick. There was something in Enya's eyes that told me she could get used to this.

Now you might be wondering, "Jo, why the heck are you giving me this giant backstory on your childhood trauma and the childhood of your doggos, and now talking about ice cream? Isn't this a story about your car accident and recovery??" Well, yes and no. Yes, I believe the purpose for this book is to help others through our story of the incident but having the backstory on not only how I got here, but how Enya got here as well is very important. Enya didn't grow up like other dogs as you now know. She grew up in the same messy environment as I did, with the fears and anxieties we dealt with in the aftermath of it all.

This was something huge that Enya continued to teach me. She began to face fears and show me that those fears were necessary for growth, even if we had to do these things scared. Elizabeth Elliot puts it this way: "Sometimes fear does not subside and you must do it afraid." [3] I love that. It reminds me so completely of Enya's personality and mantra for life. She lived that out every single day. In the months that followed Gilly's passing, Enya became a car maniac. She would wake up in the morning and bark for us until we took her for a drive to the park, the beach, to get ice cream, or a puppuccino from Starbucks. For a while I thought she just wanted to go to the destinations, but after a while, I think Devin and I both realized that the car was actually her favorite part.

She would stick her head as far as she could outside the window and live for the wind in her floofy ears. We were getting to a point where she would make us take her out for a minimum of three trips a day. (Spoiled? Nah, she deserved every one of those adventures.)

And the crazy thing is that Enya never became depressed after losing her brother. She began going everywhere with us, from grocery shopping, game nights at friend's houses, and even on road trips for little getaways. Something that was once so terrifying in her life soon became her favorite thing. She reminds me of that verse in the Bible where what was meant for evil actually turned into something that God used for good.

*"You intended to harm me, but God intended it for good. To accomplish what is now being done, the saving of many lives." Genesis 50:20*

You see, I think the atmosphere Enya and myself grew up in told us that the world wasn't a safe place, and we were supposed to be afraid of anything and everything. We avoided parks and drives because it could mean danger. But at that rate, we'd go back home to a place that was also not safe and held many dangers behind closed doors. It seemed that the enemy used this all as stepping-stones to get footholds in while my family grew to just accept it as normal. But when I look at it all now, none of that is "normal." We aren't intended to live in fear, and the things that the enemy used to harm my family and cause all kinds of division and destruction while hurting so many of us—in the end, it actually ended up being used for good, and I can see how God has turned it around for Himself.

I see a huge part of that in Enya and the way she stepped out into those car adventures and fell into that routine so easily. It was like she was throwing off the old way of things and embracing the new life God was putting in front of us. Before that, we were still learning to live life after Mom's passing. Mom had passed after a strenuous battle of colon cancer just the year before Gilly passed away. And while all of that is a whole other story in itself, I can say today I'm also very grateful for the lessons learned through all the hard battles growing up with her, and the time taking care of her in her final days. There was restoration and healing, and even though that didn't erase all the past, I'm thankful for the bits of repairs that were able to be made in the end of her life. From that point on, though, gears shifted in the lives of our family, and I don't think any of us knew what life was supposed to look like now.

I think Enya teaching us to step out into scary things really helped us embrace new freedoms and show us new ways of living beyond the walls of fear we hid behind for so long. She taught us that fear and difficult challenges were inevitable, yes, but we could still have the joy of the Lord in spite of them. Life will always have things we can't control in it, but that doesn't mean we can't have adventures and enjoy creating memories with loved ones in the midst of it.

*****

*"Feel the fear but do it anyway."*[4] *-Susan Jeffers*

In May of 2020 (almost two years before our car accident), after just celebrating Enya's fourteenth birthday with a pool party celebration, the days following, she began acting a bit off. She still wanted to go running and sprinting with me every day, but at night through her big giant smile, I saw something seemed wrong. She began developing a cough that lingered on for a few days before I told Devin that I think it was time I took her into the vet for a checkup.

Nervous to my core, I went through every possibility in my mind of the things it could be. But overall, it was hard to really consider that something serious was going on with the amount of energy and normalcy she still had in her everyday life. After running multiple tests and scans for hours on end, the vet later confronted us with the news that a mass had developed on Enya's thyroid, and it was indeed thyroid cancer.

My heart was shattered, and all the pieces were falling into my stomach, slicing wherever they pleased. I honestly had the hardest time believing them because she showed no visible signs of having cancer. My sweet pup who had, in just the course of a few months, turned from being scared of everything was now facing everything. Taking care of me and at my side every moment of every day was what she did, and now my fears of losing her were becoming a reality.

That next week was full of researching, phone calls, vet appointments, and switching to specialists in oncology. We found some amazing doctors that were so incredibly welcoming to Enya to their offices.

My biggest fear with putting Enya into treatments wasn't that she couldn't handle it. It was that the doctors wouldn't treat her because of her age. I'm a firm believer that people are so ageist when it comes to dogs that have a lot of years on them. And it was something I battled constantly with those surrounding Enya who didn't know her and what she was capable of. She wasn't just a dog that couldn't move and was sick and at the end.

No, every single day she ran sprints with me. Every day she asked to go get ice cream, would chase me around the house, would run and trot beside Devin while he skateboarded, would splash through the waves of the beach with me. Who would watch *The Office* whenever she was relaxing at home, who needed a stack of twenty blankets to curl up in and sleep on at night. The same pup who required her own, personal air conditioning unit and two fans to sleep up against at night. Yeah, that pup? She wasn't on her last legs. She was living her best life and had no intentions of stopping.

Over the next couple of weeks, Enya underwent anesthesia and radiation treatments to kick the tumor from her thyroid. Each visit was terrifying and difficult to have to watch Enya walk through the doors of the vet by herself. And because Covid-19 was at an all-time high, we weren't allowed inside with her. I sat every day in the parking lot of the vet's office, waiting for updates on her treatments. And every treatment, no matter how scared she walked in, how shaky or nervous she would be, she would run out with the biggest smile on her face and run up to her hoomans, waiting for our embrace. Every time we left, we'd be told that she would be more tired out than usual and that the radiation treatments would drain her energy for a bit. But not my girl.

We'd get home after her appointments and take a power nap, and within the hour, she would be begging to go out for a drive or a trip to the park. This wasn't an elderly pup; this was a miracle in my presence, showing me that hard things are thrown at us, but we can choose to sit around and pout about it, or we can get through it and not let it affect the rest of our day with the people we love. Enya's smiles were often so big after her treatments that it totally shocked us with the amount of joy she was able to have despite her circumstances. We even came up with a little saying when we would go through something hard, where we'd tell each other, "No pouts allowed" because we believed this was what Enya was teaching us through her journey of treatments.

Going through those months of watching her go through treatment, waiting for results and answers, was absolute torture. If you look on my social media pages, you'd see all the photos of Enya and the amazing attitudes she had throughout those few months. You'd see the wonderful news we found out when the radiation started working quicker than the vets had anticipated and how amazed everyone was when we found out that the tumor was eliminated almost completely within just a few months. We were amazed and so thankful God did such a miracle that we got to be a part of with our sweet pup.

In the months that followed, I often lived with new anxieties and realities of cancer coming back and fears and nightmares of losing Enya to such a terrible disease. My mind would run ramped, and my brain would get stuck on picturing having to hold her in her final moments, just like her family before, due to a cancerous tumor taking over her. This fear haunted every bit of me, even despite the miracle we had just witnessed.

My underlying anxieties and depression were getting worse as time went on. It was something I lived with for the vast majority of my life, but I felt I was high functioning enough until this point to push through the anxiety. But I started realizing a big support system I always had was Enya to get me out of bed when I couldn't do it myself. The idea that I was about to lose that support and someone I loved so much was eating me away. Our relationship was at a point I had never experienced before with my other pups, which is weird to say because I loved each of them with my whole heart as well. But I always felt like they were put in my life to be there for me. However, with Enya, she grew up being there for me, and now I was in charge of being there for her. She needed me; we needed each other and walked through our anxieties with a mutual understanding of what the other was facing in a way that words could not express. And through those anxieties, she taught me that it was okay to feel those fears and anxieties, but to push on and do the hard things anyway.

Over the next year and a half, which was between her cancer treatment recovery and our car accident, Enya faced a handful of other health issues. She tweaked her leg running a few times and was supposed to be on bed rest for months. After a week of rest, I had to contact the vet to let her know that Enya was trying to run again. She faced a scare with another mass on her chest near her heart. It was thankfully not cancerous, but she had to undergo radiation treatments again for that. But as I look back at that time, I don't ever remember Enya being sad or tired. Every day was full of a new adventure and full of smiles. Each day brought more hope and joy from her rising out of the ashes of a difficult year and being joyful at the end of the day.

So, I think that's why it was so abrupt and life-altering to have someone so full of hopes, dreams, and life to suddenly have that all taken from her. And even though I feared cancer coming back and defeating Enya, I never anticipated I would have to say goodbye to her over a FaceTime call from each of our hospital beds on opposite sides of the city. Something I didn't know was that Enya not only had a concussion from our accident, but she also broke her spine just like me. I didn't know during those couple of days of being apart from her, her health was declining while I thought she was recovering.

Something I learned while lying in that hospital bed was that Enya suffered severe injuries because she was sitting on my lap and took the brunt of our crash's impact. Enya acted as my shield, not only for my entire life from the pains of abuse and mental illness but shielded me physically and saved my life in the car that fateful night.

Remember in the first chapter how I mentioned looking down at Enya and seeing her not moving? And just a few moments later, I wrote about how I heard someone screaming for me to open the car door? And I thought someone pulled us all out of the car. Well, that all actually never happened. No one was around yet, and no one took us from the car. We learned that Devin pulled himself out of the car by dragging his entire body with a broken leg and got to the side of the road. But that voice that I heard, I often think about. How was someone not outside when I heard them so vividly??

I'm not trying to over-spiritualize this, and I'm not an over-the-top charismatic person in any sense. But what I learned about the rest of our story with getting out of the car tells me that whether it was God Himself or the voice of an angel, in some sense, someone made me aware that I needed to open that door. And after reaching for the handle, there's a gap between that reach and laying on the side of the road.

My dad told me that he was pulling out of the parking lot right behind us and was just moments behind our crash. He tells me now that he didn't even have time to panic; he just knew we were alive because as he drove up near us, he saw me carrying Enya out of the car and walking to the side of the road. I still don't recall any of this and have gone through many therapy sessions to help with struggling with the fact that I hate not being able to remember holding Enya that last time due to my mind being in shock. My therapist explained that maybe it is a sense of protection God has given me. After all, why do I want to remember such a scary and sad moment when I have so many other moments and memories of holding Enya and the joy felt in those moments?

Pain and joy can coexist, and I think it's something I may struggle with for a long time. And I often still find myself trying to remember and imagine those final moments getting to hold her. But at the same time, I'm learning that God has designed our brains in a way with the concept of being in shock; and although that's so terrifying in itself, it's something that could be bad but God has turned it around and used it for good for us.

*****

### God's Mercy

*"Living in a world with unanswered whys forces us to lean on Jesus."* [5]
-Karen Ehman

Two days after our crash, a phone was brought to me, and we said our final goodbyes to Enya over a FaceTime call. I didn't get to hold her; I didn't get to squeeze her fur or her little paw. Her passing wasn't how I pictured it at all. It wasn't supposed to be like this. I had lived in a world the last couple years in total fear and with this image in mind of having to say goodbye to her because of cancer. But now somehow this seemed worse to me. I couldn't be there with her in her final moments.

I was reading a book called *It's Not Supposed To Be This Way* by Lysa Terkeurst this morning and came across this quote that I found helpful when it comes to thoughts on this topic. Lysa writes;

*"Death is but a passageway at God's designated time for us to finally escape this broken world full of imperfections and be welcomed to the Home we've been longing for our entire lives."* [6]

This whole idea of being in control and thinking I could be in charge of how and when I would say goodbye to Enya was something I didn't realize I had such a tight grip on for so many years. And when I look at it now, I see that maybe this whole thing was actually a way that saved her from having to suffer through a long and painful passing. It reminds me of a post I had written on social media just a couple months after Enya passed away. Below a photo of Enya and I walking at the beach, during Golden hour, I write this:

*What if it was an act of God's mercy that we lost you?*

*I was challenged with this question since the day we had to say goodbye. No, it doesn't answer all of my questions, or heal the hurt of not having you here to help us recover with your smile.*

*I keep struggling with not the questioning of why we had to go through this ... but why your sweet heart had to be taken in it.*

*You didn't hurt anyone. You brought everyone joy around you.*

*You cared deeply, loved fiercely, and reminded us of defiant joy in the midst of hard things.*

*So why did you not get a second chance like we did?*

*Your boy hooman (what we referred to Devin, as when we talked to Enya) says you got such a special second chance.*

*After your brother Gilly passed away, we were terrified you would get depressed.*

*But that same day, you faced your fear of the car, jumped in for a ride to the park, and never looked back.*

*You beat cancer, you beat other major health issues and other hard things. For nearly two years, you turned a sad situation into a motivation to live each moment full of joy.*

*So, I guess I wish you got a third chance, but I was also so scared every single day of the cancer coming back, or some health problem hurting you.*

*But now you don't have to do that.*

*You got to run just a few minutes before the crash at the park.*

*So as much as I want to bury my head in your furry chest, take you to get more pupichinos, and for us to get to take you on all the new adventures, I will try to start leaning into Christ and that He allowed this to happen, and that's the most loving thing He could do.*

*He isn't just concerned with justice. He is just. He isn't just loving. He is love. He isn't just merciful. He is mercy.*

*So, with Him being love, even if I don't understand, and even if it doesn't fill the hole in our hearts of us missing you, I will begin to trust in our God that He is loving you so deeply right now and that this was the most merciful thing He could do.*

*This month without you hurts my heart so deeply. I love you, Sweet Enya baby.*

*I miss chasing Golden hour with you. But I know my Golden girl is running on those Golden Streets.*

*Forever missing you."*

I miss her every single day and often look over my shoulder, expecting her to be right behind me following like she always was. I don't know if I'll ever get out of that habit. But I'm learning how merciful God is and that maybe He intended this all as a way for Enya to not suffer anymore and to be merciful to her in her final days. I know He's holding her … or, better yet, I bet she's refusing to be held and running around, begging for food, on the golden streets now. I know that she is with the All loving, All just, and All merciful God right now, free of cancer, pain, and heartache. My heart aches for her, but I realize it shouldn't because she is the happiest and healthiest she has ever been. Her joy, I bet, is through the clouds.

I close out this chapter with this final, little story. While recovering in the hospital, my sister Bry told me about this conversation she had with her son (my nephew) Bear. He was five years old at this time, and it amazes me how God can use such a small child in such a powerful way. This conversation helped my heart while grieving the loss of Enya.

Bry told me that Bear was watching a Sunday school lesson on the TV. The Bible story he was learning about on that particular day was about how Jesus died on the cross for us to take away our sins. How Jesus sacrificed Himself for us because He loved us so much. Bear then turned around to his mom and said, "That's like what Enya did for Auntie Jo to save her!"

Every time I think about this, I can't help but break down. Enya has left a legacy of unconditional love and sacrifice that no matter how young you are, you can see and understand. She will always be remembered for the joy she brought others and the joy she had despite her circumstances. I will forever hold dear to my heart, my baby girl Enya. Enya is the pup that gave her life for mine. *"An immeasurable tragedy: I will love you for the rest of my life and you will not be here for any of it."*[7] *~Chloe Frayne*

As a side bar: if you would like some encouragement for your day, or you'd like to see some photos of Enya's journey and joys throughout the years, you can type in the hashtag online #Enyasbigventures and #braveheartEnya. I'm encouraged and so thankful for these special memories and joys to look back on, finding encouragement through Enya to keep going on for her.

# Chapter 4: Distance Between Hospital Rooms

*"Two are better than one, because they have a good return for their labor: If either of them falls down, on can help the other up. But pity anyone who falls and has no one to help them up."Ecclesiastes 4:9-10*

I WAS TALKING TO Devin one day about how I don't understand that there are some couples in this world, seemingly most couples in fact, who do not tell each other everything. They could go a whole day without saying anything to each other or telling one another about the events that occurred in their lives throughout that day. I told him, "I don't understand ... I literally tell you every detail, down to if I got a paper cut that day!" I know, it's cheesy to a lot of people, but this is how we work ... this is and always has been us.

I think this is why in our now five years of marriage, and over eight years of being together, we have formulated and been able to sort through the mountains of life with such good communication. Because we know everything about each other, the books of our brains are open wide to one other. So, when we were faced with undoubtedly the biggest hurdle in our lives, and we were separated during the ordeal, it goes without saying we struggled hardcore with loneliness and uncertainty of how to walk through this valley before each of us.

We were on the same hike, but at different trail heads, with different boulders and hurdles in our ways. Having to make major medical decisions without getting to talk with each other first, struggling with fear and uncertainty without being able to hold hands through it, having to go through something so extreme together while being apart was something I don't wish on anyone in this life.

We both encountered multiple surgeries, and not being able to be present with the other was so difficult. Having to cry together on Facetime while we said goodbye to our pup and not be able to hold each other through that was one of the deepest hurts of our hearts. There was something so difficult about having your person who no one can prevent you from seeing was suddenly separated from you and not having any control over it. I think I asked nearly every nurse and doctor to put us in the same room, or to load one of us up in a wheelchair to be wheeled to the other's room.

It wasn't until one week after the accident that we finally got to hold each other and cry in each other's arms. Before that, I was wheeled by Devin's room once, thanks to a kind nurse who decided breaking the rules was worth it, so that I could wave to Devin before I went into spinal surgery. The sense of having your world cave in around you and feel like you're losing control, while also not having control over being with your significant other, is a different kind of pain.

At the time of our accident, we had been married for almost five years. And in those five years, we had never been apart for a night. That wasn't always easy: sometimes being together involved skipping events, Devin driving home from somewhere he was called to work hours away and offered lodging by his work. But he always turned it down and made the trek back to me so that we could be together. I know a lot of people don't understand that and don't see the harm in being away from each other for a night or two.

And maybe it isn't that big of a deal. But when it wasn't completely necessary and if we had other options, we chose them. Because this is what we signed up for, to become one flesh, and to do everything in our power to live life together rather than apart. This means sharing everything from talking about your day, to being able to lay down, side by side, together in bed at night. This is something we have always cherished, and something we will never take for granted, especially after being separated for nearly a month.

This may seem like a bit of an odd chapter. But I think it's an important factor in our story of the crash. We've always been big on promoting marriage and sharing in anything and everything together, and so finding ways to have to work around that, while being forced apart, is a chunk of the journey we've been on. In a lot of ways, this taught us to seek Christ even more. Though we didn't have each other physically there, we were able to deepen our faith in God and grow in ways through the journey of loneliness and apartness.

I think something we both kept hearing from those around us was how God was going to use our story for something good. This was a big encouragement that got me through a lot of dark moments while lying in that ICU bed. Encouraging each other in that belief was really crucial in getting us through that dark climb. Our phone calls to each other were brief and, honestly, I have trouble remembering them to this day; and I know Devin struggles with this too.

Because we were both so heavily medicated and constantly in and out of surgeries, we were both exhausted but still pursuing each other whenever we could.

I read this quote recently:

*"What if, this time, God desires to make something completely brand new? Right now. On this side of eternity. No matter how shattered our circumstances may seem?"*[1] *- Lysa Terkeurst*

Now, being on the other side of that hospital separation, and back to spending every possible moment together, has been extremely helpful in our recovery. There's something about learning how to relearn to sleep in the same bed as someone you've slept with for years that was a comical yet difficult challenge I never would have anticipated before our crash. Our first night together after I was released from rehab and back home with Devin, we couldn't hold each other like we used to. Pillows were propped up on all sides of either of us, holding up our limbs and supporting broken places our bodies couldn't hold up on their own just yet.

There was an unspoken rule about not bumping the other because we understood the serious level of pain the other would encounter if moved even in the slightest way. Devin had to sleep on the right side of the bed; I had to sleep on the left. And up until this point, it was always the opposite. I could only get in and out of bed by rolling onto my right side. His leg required him to get in and out of bed, and sometimes even needed to hang on the left side. This was new and scary and weird. I couldn't hold his hand because my left arm was in a sling. We were finally together, yet still felt so far apart without being able to hold and support each other in the ways that we were so used to before.

I remember so many nights of lying in bed and just sobbing. I was so frustrated and defeated by our new realities, and it seemed like this would be our lives forever. I often spiraled, in full-blown panics, and Devin had to learn new ways to help calm and talk me through without being able to hold me tightly in his safe embrace. Looking back, I am still in complete awe at where we are today. This isn't our reality anymore. Yes, we still struggle hardcore with getting comfortable at night, and we definitely have to still be strategic to not bump the other one's injuries when adjusting. But that nightmare came to an end: it was long and difficult and seemingly never-ending. Devin kept telling me it was temporary, when my mind was telling me it was eternal.

I heard this quote the other day, and it felt really relatable to the physical challenges we faced on this journey:

*"Healing isn't taking the fast lane down the highway.*
*Healing is taking back roads with potholes and dead ends.*
*But I will get there. I will."*[2] *~Jennae Cecelia*

If I would have heard this during those first few months of bedrest and recovery, I probably would've slapped the person telling me. I didn't believe it. And even now, being so far into recovery, I still struggle when the pain days come at all-time highs, or when I think of the things Devin and I will never be able to do again because of physical challenges we face now. It's frustrating and so easy to get stuck there.

It was difficult to pray about healing and recovery while at the same time grieving the life lost that would never come back. And I think that's when God started teaching me that just because there are difficult realities, this doesn't mean we have to live our lives in hopelessness. I'll write more on my struggles through hopelessness and the depths of depression I've fallen into from rehab to now. But for now, I want to focus on the fact that we can wrestle with real-life realities and new challenges that may go on for a, while simultaneously trusting that God has a purpose for growing our faith through the unknowns.

If you're like me, I don't find the idea of praying to be difficult. But I struggle with praying about big things and trying to be real with God; and then my mind wanders into concern for those troubles I'm trying to pray about. And instead of handing them over to God, my mind begins to go down its own path on trying to solve things on its own. I know I can't be the only one that has a hard time with this. In fact, I've heard it said: *"If you find that your mind wanders while you're praying, maybe you should pray about what your mind keeps wandering to."*[3] -(Anonymous)

I think there are two points off about this. The first is that if our minds are wandering while we are praying, our minds are essentially telling us that we don't quite trust God enough to be able to release it completely from our grasp into His. So, there is the side of praying about that, and not only the situation, but praying about a change of heart in the midst of it so that this pattern in the lack of trust in Christ does not continue to leak into other areas of our lives.

The second is that we must learn to talk to God as a conversation compared to our initial thought of talking at Him. What I mean by that is that we should be telling Him everything. Like, literally, He wants to hear it all. Remember how I said earlier that I'll tell Devin something as small as the paper cut I got earlier that day? It's the same thought process with Christ. He's right beside us and eager to hear about our struggles and our wins in life. I think it's such a powerful tool that we get to learn while walking through marriage and the idea of sharing everything together. It's just a small glimpse into the interaction and being able to have that connection with our Father as well as our spouse. God wants to share in the life He has given us.

I learned a lot about the concept of sharing from the book *A Severe Mercy* by Sheldon Vanaken. This concept of sharing is something that has been a tool and a major building block in our marriage. When we first began dating, we knew that there were different interests we each had. And rather than throwing our relationship out the window, like this world so easily tries to tell us, we used it to become closer to each other and grow together.

Devin likes video games, while I hardly knew how to hold a controller the correct way. I was playing professional softball for a while there, and Devin knew close to nothing about the sport. We could've chosen to live our lives separately, but we knew the other loved those things, so learning about those things meant learning more about each other. We first started making this decision through two years of dating, and even as our wedding day came, we each included in our vows that we would continue to share in everything and try new things with the other always.

Sheldon Vanauken puts it this way:

> *We talked deeply, not about the already-settled matter of secrets, but about justice between lovers and about how to make love endure. What emerged from our talk was nothing less, we believed, than the central "secret" of enduring love: sharing.*

> *"Look," we said, "what is it that draws two people into closeness and love? Of course there's the mystery of physical attraction, but beyond that it's the things they share. We both love strawberries and ships and collies and poems and all beauty, and all those things bind us together. Those sharings just happened to be but what we must do now is share everything. Everything! If one of us likes anything, there must be something to like in it—and the other one must find it."*[4]

So, you see, something that God was teaching us so early on in our story with one another actually ended up being a big foundation in learning to walk through recovery together (no pun intended.) It was a stepping-stone in learning a new way to communicate and grow with Christ through this difficult chapter we were facing. It meant talking to Him about everything, even if that meant nothing would change in our circumstances. It meant surrendering control by learning to talk without expecting anything in return from Him. It meant blindly trusting Him to hold my fears and hurts in His hands, knowing that He would do whatever He saw best for our circumstances, whether that meant being paralyzed or if it meant learning to walk again.

By sharing my heart, I got to share in a new aspect of my relationship with Christ; this is what sharing in marriage has taught us. And I had no idea that God would use it in our worst-case scenario of life through our accident. I love the verse in Isaiah 48:17 that says:

*"This is what the LORD says—your Redeemer, the Holy One of Israel: 'I am the LORD your God, who teaches you what is best for you, who directs you in the way you should go.'"*

I find this encouraging because we can see that the way God was teaching the people of Israel was for the things that were going to come to pass in their future. He was directing and guiding them—He was growing them in ways and providing them with the tools they would need to have endurance and be prepared for situations down the line in their lives.

So, I want to encourage you reading this to pay attention to the things He is teaching you right now—even in the seemingly mundane days of life. The way He used people and taught people then, He will do now in your life too. He is the same God and is preparing you on this journey of life for the mountain coming that might just be a strenuous climb. He's giving you tools to carry in your hiking pack that will guide you and help your endurance along the way. Don't take them lightly because you have no idea what is in store for you! You don't have to understand it all right now, but learning to be obedient in what He has in front of you, without trying to run ahead or do things in our own control, becomes crucial to confronting anxieties in our lives.

*"When I understand that everything happening to me is to make me more Christ like, it resolves a great deal of anxiety."*[5] - A.W. Tozer

# Chapter 5: Final ICU Days, Rehabilitation & Hopelessness

*"We are not being led to see God in our stories but to see our stories in God."*[1] *- Eugene Paterson*

SPINAL SURGERY WAS ONE of the single, most terrifying experiences I'll hopefully never have to go through again. It's a tricky thing to explain when I have trouble even remembering all the events of that day because the gaps of being heavily medicated are there instead. I know I was scared, so a nurse gave me a Xanax to try to relax. Instead of relaxing, my heart just continued to beat fast, but I was too tired to tell anyone I was scared. So, I guess in a sense the medication worked in that weird way. I remember being in pre-op and talking with a nurse who was going over the details of the surgery about to take place, along with the anesthesiologist, who would be in the operating room and in charge of putting me to sleep.

    I remember the nurse being especially kind and supportive. Though her face was mostly covered by her mask, her eyes showed a deep kindness as she looked into mine and spoke words to try to keep me calm, as I was crying for fear of all that was about to take place. She talked about how she knew Devin and had heard our story of what had happened to us. Apparently, we were a hot topic going on in the news and buzzing through the hospital through doctors and nurses. I felt a little like a celebrity, just not in the way one really hopes to become famous.

She told me about how sweet Devin was and how she also had prepared him for one of his surgeries that week. She talked about how he wouldn't stop telling her about me, which filled me with a lot of joy to know that he was proud to call me his and eager to tell others about me, even while prepping for a scary surgery himself. I don't remember too many other details of that surgery day. I know I didn't handle the anesthesia and waking up well. That's no surprise; I never do. I remember it was successful and no further damage was done to my spine, which was a huge relief. I know that morning, I expressed to those around me who prayed over me that I was terrified of never walking again, but I knew God was going to use all this, whether I was paralyzed or whether I'd be able to walk again. I was in a lot of pain, but also thankful. I was grieving every moment of being awake with the loss of our pup and having to say goodbye on the phone just the day before.

After two weeks in the hospital, talk of discharge and what was to come began to play out. Devin was released home just a couple of days before, while I was directed to be put into a rehabilitation facility. To this day, it's still confusing and not fully understood why Devin was also not transferred to rehabilitation. He went through two major surgeries to put his shattered femur and ankle back together with multiple screws, a metal rod, and many staples. He was directed that absolutely no weight was to be put on his left leg for the next several months. So, it was odd why he wasn't also sent somewhere to have helping hands to guide him through living with this extensive injury.

Two weeks in the hospital for me, and the swelling had finally gone down enough in my collarbone for them to perform surgery on it. I remember waking up that morning and my breakfast being brought into my room. Nothing was scheduled for the day at that point, so it was just another day in the ICU. After finishing a banana, I had multiple nurses come in and question me on why I was eating. Confused for a moment, then they explained I was supposed to be booked for a last-minute surgery on my clavicle. They took away my food tray, and my surgery was pushed back into the afternoon so the banana I apparently shouldn't have eaten wouldn't affect the surgery.

In the hours that I waited for the go-ahead to be sent in, I remember being the most conscious I had been in the last couple of weeks. Because of that, I understood that surgery was coming and was very aware this was going to be another hurdle that I would have to jump over in our recovery road. I was scared after already being in so much pain, and essentially just having to accept that more was coming was debilitating. But more pain had to come in order to truly heal all the way. I couldn't just continue laying there without being put back together in my broken places. That wouldn't allow true healing to take place.

It reminds me now of this story I heard once in a book and how it compares to God allowing pain in our lives in order to grow us in Him. In Lee Strobel's book *The Case for Faith*, he is interviewing a philosophy professor and writer named John Kreeft. Lee Strobel asks him to explain how there can be an all-loving God, yet have so much pain and suffering in the world. His answer is absolutely mind-blowing. He says:

Kreeft thought for a moment. "Look at it this way," he said. "Would you agree that the difference between us and God is greater than the difference between us and, say, a bear?"

I nodded.

"Okay, then, imagine a bear in a trap and a hunter who out of sympathy, wants to liberate him. He tries to win the bear's confidence, but he can't do it, so he has to shoot the bear full of drugs. The bear, however thinks this is an attack and the hunter is trying to kill him. He doesn't realize that this is done out of compassion.

"Then, in order to get the bear out of the trap, the hunter has to push him further into the trap to release the tension of the spring. If the bear were semi-conscious at this point, he would be even more convinced the hunter is his enemy who was out to cause him suffering and pain. But the bear would be wrong. He reaches his incorrect conclusion because he's not a human being."

Kreft let the illustration sink in for a moment. "Now," he concluded, "how can anyone be certain that's not an analogy between us and God? I believe God does the same to us sometimes, and we can't comprehend why he does it any more than the bear can understand the motivations of the hunter. As the bear could have trusted the hunter, so we can trust God."[2]

I still don't have all the answers to the questions I've asked God and why we went through this whole journey. But now that it's nearly a year later, and my head isn't full of medications that determine the consciousness of my mind, I can wrap my head around the idea a bit better that maybe our circumstances were a lot like the bear trap. Maybe in our lives, we were in some kind of trap or situation, and the only way God saw fit to help us out was to seemingly allow this all to happen. And maybe He was really helping us through all of it, even though at times it just seemed like we were being pushed deeper into a painful trap.

I can say very honestly that in the evening I got out of that surgery; I was in the most excruciating physical pain I'd ever been in my life. I had nurses and doctors surrounding me, confused as to why I was in so much pain. They explained it made zero sense and that the amount of pain medication in my system was to a level that would have put anyone else my age in a coma. We'll circle back to the whole problem with medications in a later chapter, because I have a lot to say on all that. But all this to say, I felt the surgery caused greater pain than I was having before. How is it that my collarbone was completely cracked off in multiple places, and that was more comfortable than being put back together and repaired?

Oftentimes in life, we will face tears like that defenseless bear. We are cautious and skeptical of this hunter who we don't know all the details about. But by faith, we can trust that in the end, He really is just trying to help us out. *"And the God of all grace who called you to his eternal glory in Christ, after you have suffered a little while, will himself restore you and make you strong, firm and steadfast"* (1 Pet. 5:10).

*"Consider it pure joy, my brothers and sisters, whenever you face trials of many kinds, because you know that the testing of your faith produces perseverance. Let perseverance finish its world so that you may be mature and complete, not lacking anything" (James 1:2-4).*

*****

## Rehabilitation

*"If someone says you can't do it; do it twice and take pictures."* [3]
*- (Anonymous)*

Up until this point, I thought the car accident would be the hardest thing I'd ever have to go through. As it turns out, living life after that was the hardest. Being transferred from the hospital to a rehabilitation facility was difficult all on its own. I still couldn't walk, as after my spinal surgery, any time I would try to lift my head, my blood pressure would drop to dangerously low levels. This continued every day when the team of physical therapists and nurses would try to teach me how to stand and learn to use my legs again. This was unsuccessful in the hospital, and I wasn't able to learn to walk again for a while when in rehab.

So being transferred to a place almost an hour away from home, where Devin now was, quickly became a new worst-case scenario. I was scared and hating the idea of having to stay in an unknown place alone, especially so far away from anyone I knew. I didn't know if I'd ever walk again. In fact, when I finally got settled into my new room in the facility, I remember having a major breakdown, as the negative thoughts crept in and overtook my mind. I couldn't move on my own. I had limited strength, and so many restrictions just even in the bed that any movement either hurt or terrified me that I would re-break my spine.

Up until this point, I was on a catheter in the hospital because my bladder was damaged, and I didn't know how to pee on my own anymore. But now even if I did, I couldn't get myself to a bathroom even if I wanted to. As it turns out, one of the factors of getting permission to be released to leave rehab was learning how to do things on my own again. And as they took away the catheter and explained that my body needed to learn these things again, I quickly decided in my mind that I would never get out of rehab. A team of nurses worked together to get my back brace on and sit me up. I was dizzy, my ears were ringing, and I was on the verge of passing out. My blood pressure was too low to stand, and I hadn't gotten my bearings with my legs yet. The nurses loaded me up on the most bizarre-looking device that would transfer me from my bed and into the bathroom.

I thought it was humiliating enough to not know how to physically go to the bathroom anymore on my own. Turns out that it actually got worse when people place you on a toilet and stand by to make sure you learn and don't fall along the way. If nothing else, I definitely learned a lot of humility in that rehabilitation room. There's nothing to be proud of when you need to ask for help in areas like this. And it was only the beginning.

Due to Covid-19 restrictions, I was only allowed one visitor a day and for limited hours. This was defeating, as I already had struggled so much with being lonely in the hospital when the room would empty after visiting hours. Now to know I would be spending even more time alone was a new mountain I did not want to face. Devin came down every single day—he wasn't allowed to drive yet with being on so many medications. I appreciated his eagerness to see me every day, and despite having to face the car rides that were so scary after everything and the pain of sitting through discomfort with his injuries in the car, he came in smiling and happy to be there for me each afternoon.

We were both exhausted, and time together always flew by. We both were at risk for blood clots, since neither of us could walk, and so the result was each of us having to have a shot in our stomach every day in order to protect us from them. Devin's mom was trained and gave them to him each day at home. And in rehab, I quickly became fed up with getting poked and going through this routine every day. I think that was the first moment I became motivated to recover. Up until then, the grief and frustration were towering over me, and I couldn't see any way around this valley in front of me. But I was tired of the shots. Forget the pain of my other surgeries, and everything else we were dealing with; this was one thing I was getting rid of, the shots.

I remember asking my nurse a couple of days into rehab what I needed to do in order to stop needing the stomach shots. I don't remember the exact number today, but I was required to take at least a couple hundred steps a day in order to decrease my risk of blood clots. Within those twenty-four hours, I was walking again. Now I don't believe that was me or in my own power. I do believe that my mind was fed up and wanted to have control of at least one thing in the midst of everything else flying out of control around me.

But I know that God was working and healing, and the people that were praying for us all across the country were a part of this healing process. I was still in pain, and my blood pressure was unmanageable and dangerously low each and every step I took. But it was better than the first day. Healing was happening, God was moving, and I wasn't the only one seeing it. The nurses in the facility were in absolute shock. I had one come into my room randomly late one evening, as I was beginning to doze off from the medications kicking in.

I remember being a bit stunned when she started the conversation by asking me what my religion was. This opened up a door to be able to share that I was a Christ follower, and that people were praying for me to heal and be able to walk again. She wasn't a Christian, but I could see the Holy Spirit working in this conversation, and she ended the conversation by telling me it made no sense that I was walking again and less than forty-eight hours of being within the facility. She told me to tell those who were praying for me to walk again to also pray for my collarbone to heal so that I could use my arm again someday as well. She believed in the power of prayer because she got to witness firsthand God's healing in a seemingly impossible situation.

This was the first moment that God began stirring in my heart and telling me, "Jo, without this accident, you would have never gotten to meet these nurses or any of these people and share about Me with them." This is what got me through the hardest moments. The reality that this was a ministry and a chance that I could share God's love and power through our story kept me going.

Over the next eight days, I worked hard and pushed my body to the new limits I had to adjust to. I'd always been good at pushing through physical pain. Growing up an athlete, my body was pushed far beyond its limits when playing competitive softball games in 115-degree weather and often nearly five games in a day. This was something I could, or so I thought I could, handle. But when your body is broken and torn apart, needing to be rebuilt and put back together, it becomes a new body. I quickly realized that this was going to be a new journey of learning to live in a body that felt completely foreign to the one I had spent the last twenty-five years living in.

In order to graduate from rehabilitation, I was required to learn new skills and be approved and signed off on in multiple areas of therapy. First there was speech therapy. That was the first one I passed quickly; the only note was that I would have some recovering to do in my mind from my concussion. Next was occupational therapy, which was where I was taught how to learn daily tasks that I once took for granted being able to accomplish them so easily; now it was a struggle just to get myself dressed in the morning.

Each morning, my occupational therapist would come in, hand me my set of clothes, and I was in charge of getting myself ready for the day. The first day of rehab, I was immediately humbled when handed my clothes, and I laid flat on my back, with staples in my back, unable to twist or lift myself, unable to hold my head up with my low blood pressure, and my left arm in a sling due to no function from my collarbone to my fingers. So being told "get dressed" seemed impossible. I think that first morning took nearly two hours of me attempting to get dressed, only to end up giving up and needing help. So, I wasn't going to graduate from that one so easily.

Over the next week, tools were brought to me that were helpful with learning to put on socks and grabbers to help me reach for things on the ground or out of reach. With the help of these tools, everyday life looked different, but I was learning new ways to get through them. On top of this therapy, I was scheduled every day for physical therapy, where I'd be held up by my back brace, a cane, and a belt for my therapist to hold onto, and I'd walk as many steps as my blood pressure and back would allow. In the gym, I would work on machines with one arm to keep my blood pumping and build strength back up in limbs that hadn't done much in the last several weeks.

On top of this, I still needed to graduate from social therapy with meeting new people and getting to know staff, as well as psychotherapy, where a psychologist would come in most days to discuss my overall mental health and talk through the events of everything I was facing. My mental health and the effects that the crash had on it will be something I dive into in another chapter. But it was something that really did take the center stage of rehab and was a constant, everyday battle I faced. Throughout each day, I would struggle with keeping my eyes on Jesus and staying fixed on His purpose set before me. I knew He wanted me to be an example of His love to the nurses, doctors, and other patients around me. But there was a very real enemy I was facing, and I'll never forget my psychologist putting a name to it in our very first session.

Hopelessness. She told me, "Jo, you seem like you are living in hopelessness." And I very much was. Although I was on fire and reaching out every chance I could to share the love of Christ and talk about Bible studies, the gospel, God's healing, and encouraging others to get to know Him, I still went back to my room after each therapy, and in the lonesomeness and quietness of that room, I faced this lack of hope. I was at rock bottom, but then after hitting that and attempting to stand up, the floor caved in, and I fell in rock bottom's basement again.

Life was looking very different from anything I had once pictured. Before the accident, Devin and I were in search of a house that we could purchase as our very first home. We often dreamed of the yard we wanted for Enya to be able to run around in. The hopes of having a beautiful staircase that leads up to our bedroom in a loft. We had been working hard for several years to make this dream a reality, but there were so many potholes and curves along the way. And each time we thought we found the way to success, it somehow didn't work out, and the rug was pulled out from under us. But then, less than two weeks before our crash, we were on the hunt again. We had brushed ourselves off and stood up again, hoping and looking for this home to call our own.

But now, not only did this dream get postponed, it wasn't even a possibility for an unseen period of time. Devin was at home being taken care of by his mom, who was his full-time caretaker, and who would also become mine when I was released. Unable to do most everyday things on our own, we quickly realized that searching for a house to live in on our own was not a reality. But it wasn't just the pause put on this dream that was getting to me. It was now that those things we had once pictured, and the characteristics we had always talked about, were no longer in our future.

The dream of a big backyard for Enya to run around and play in was no longer a dream, because Enya was no longer here. The dream of a loft was no longer physically possible with Devin being in a wheelchair, and myself with a cane. The hurdles and hoops we worked so hard to overcome for years now, and just when we thought we got through them all, suddenly a mountain got thrown on the course and we lacked the ability to even begin the climb with our injuries. So yes, that word hopelessness; that fit the picture in my mind perfectly. I had given up on those dreams and accepted that our new lives would be full of grief, physical and emotional pain, and a lot of baggage to carry along the way.

But somehow, putting a name to it began to stir things in my mind and heart that I didn't want there. I struggled with this idea that I was presenting myself, as a follower of Christ, as someone who didn't have any hope, when the one I wanted to share about with others is our Living Hope. There were many days where I didn't want to push through. I wanted to give up and, honestly, just moments of hoping I wouldn't wake up. But through those moments, God kept reaching down. He kept picking me up and placing me down on a solid place to stand, which was Him. He reminded me and encouraged me to press on for Him, so that others could be encouraged and know Him through our story. That's not to say I stopped struggling then nor now with hopelessness. It is a very real battle I face daily that Christ goes to war within my heart and mind.

But along the way, His Spirit reminded me that these sufferings were necessary to grow my faith. They were there to grow my character and put to the test the hope I had set in Christ before life fell apart. In Romans 5:35, it says this:

> *Not only so, but we also glory in our sufferings, because we know that suffering produces perseverance, perseverance, character; and character, hope. And hope does not put us to shame, because God's love has been poured out into our hearts through the Holy Spirit, who has been given to us.*

One way I was able to tangibly grab on to this idea of even considering having hope again was in one of my therapy sessions. My psychologist told me, "Jo, you remind me of a phoenix. You have gone through so much but have still come up from the ashes." If you aren't familiar with the phoenix, it's an analogy of the phoenix bird who goes through fire and flames, but even when brought down into ashes, it rises again even stronger than before.

Sometimes Christ will allow us to go through fires in this life. But He will not let them overtake us, and He sure as heck doesn't make them walk through the flames alone. He does this so that we search for Him amongst the smoke and despite the pain around us. He grows our faith, and our perseverance is stretched and grown when we learn to stop giving in and accepting the pain of defeat. Our faith is matured when we stop frantically searching for Him on the other side of the flames and realize that all we have to do is look to our side, where He was standing all along amidst the flames around us.

> "But now, this is what the LORD says—
> he who created you, Jacob,
> He who formed you Israel;
> "Do not fear, for I have redeemed you;
> I have summoned you by name; you are mine.
> When you pass through the waters, I will be with you;
> And when you pass through the rivers, they will not sweep over you.
> When you walk through the fire, you will not be burned;
> The flames will not set you ablaze.
> For I am the LORD your God, the Holy One of Israel, your Savior..."
> Isaiah 43:1-3

After eight days in rehab, graduating from multiple therapies, and sharing more discussions and having more opportunities than I ever had before to talk about Christ, I was going cold turkey off of medications that were doing more harm than good to me. After Devin spent every afternoon coming to read with me, watch movies with me, cry with me, and then having to say goodbye at night, this was all coming to a close. Now walking out of the rehab I once had to be wheeled into, I was discharged and getting ready to be on my way home. I swore up and down throughout those weeks in the ICU and rehab that I would never get in a car again. But Christ has a way of giving you that nudge to keep going, even through the scary things, in order to experience all the good on the other side. Facing the fear of getting in the car meant getting to go back home and be in the same bed as my hubby for the first time in nearly a month. This car ride, no matter how terrifying, was not going to stop me.

*"What came first, the phoenix or the flame?"* [4] *– J.K. Rowling*

# Chapter 6: Recovery At Home

*"What if broken dreams are not a waste, but compost?"* [1]
*-@motherwwortandrose*

I STARTED THIS BIBLE study today that is centered around the armor of God. One of the passages that the homework had us read took place in 2 Kings 6:15-17. The verses say this:

*When the servant of the man of God got up and went out early the next morning, an army with horses and chariots had surrounded the city, "oh no, my lord! What shall we do?" the servant asked.*

*"Don't be afraid," the prophet answered. "Those who are with us are more than those who are with them."*

*And Elisha prayed, "Open his eyes, LORD, so that he may see." Then the LORD opened the servant's eyes, and he looked and saw the hills full of horses and chariots of fire around Elisha.*

This was a really eye-opening (maybe a little pun is intended here) passage for me, as I prepared to write this chapter on the beginning of our recovery journey once we got back home. What I didn't realize then, and that I see now, is that there was and is a war going on around me. While I was aware that God provided spiritual forces to protect and shield us in our crash, I didn't go as far as to think that the war was still on and taking place all around us. I thought that since we survived the battle of the crash, the hospital, and time apart in rehab, things were beginning to, hopefully, slow down. But in all reality, the war was just getting started.

I think, like the servant in this story in 2 Kings, I struggle with just focusing on the physical things going on around me, forgetting that there is also an even greater war that is invisible and taking place right in front of me. In my Bible study homework, it closed on the point that we need to be praying to Christ to open our eyes to see not only the things that we see in front of us, but also to pray that God reveals the invisible war going on around us. Not so that we live in fear, but so that we can be prepared and on alert. There's so much of me that wishes I would've been doing this study during that start of recovery so I could prepare my heart and mind for the battle taking place.

But now that I am more aware and on guard, I have the tools to take on the full armor of God and continue to fight in this war more prepared and suited in things that will protect me. His armor will not fail me.

> *Finally, be strong in the Lord, and in his mighty power. Put on the full armor of God, so that you can take your stand against the devil's schemes. For our struggle is not against flesh and blood, but against rulers, against authorities, against the powers of this dark world and against the spiritual forces of the evil in the heavenly realms. Therefore put on the full armor of God, so that when the day of evil comes, you may be able to stand your ground, and after you have done everything, to stand. Stand firm then, with the belt of truth buckled around your waist, with the breastplate of righteousness in place, and with your feet fitted with the*

*readiness that comes from the gospel of peace. In addition to all this, take up the shield of faith, which you can extinguish all the flaming arrows of the evil one. Take the helmet of salvation and the sword of the Spirit, which is the Word of God. And pray in the Spirit on all occasions, with all kinds of prayers and requests. With this in mind, be alert and always keep on praying for all the Lord's people.*
*Ephesians 6:10-18*

As author and Bible study teacher Priscilla Shirer, whose *Armor of God* study curriculum I'm currently studying, says:

*Your real enemy—the devil—wants you to ignore the spiritual reality behind the physical one. Because as long as you are focused on what you can see with your physical eyes, he can continue to run rampant underneath the surface. The more you disregard him, the more damage he is free to do. The enemy may be invisible, but he is not fictional."*[2]

Once the ideal shock of the accident was over with, and Devin and I were in our own room and own bed again, I thought the hardest part was over. But in the months that followed, we were engaged in some of the hardest physical, emotional, mental, and spiritual battles we'd ever been in. Physical pain has a way of taking over your mind and influencing your mental state. My emotions were vulnerable and wide open to attacks from the enemy left and right. Every day, I struggled with spiraling once the pain hit its peaks. I'd go through the same cycle daily of becoming hopeless, grieving all that was lost for us, and accepting that life would forever be this major battle of grief and physical pain.

Battling the constant fears when new sensations hit was terrifying. Every time I moved and something felt different or weird in my spine, I would break down with the fear that hardware in my back broke off, or I did something by accident to damage the repairs in my body. There was the whole side of just dealing with the physical pains that follow a major accident and major surgeries. But something I never thought of was the constant uncertainty of what I was supposed to be feeling and what was actually a real danger to my body. And every moment I began to spiral, I would spiral even more, knowing that I couldn't have Enya beside me smiling and encouraging me on.

I just accepted that God allowed these things to happen—things that were some of my worst fears in life. The idea of losing Enya and Devin, or one of them getting hurt, was something I struggled with fearing for years, and every day, I attempted to control the circumstances around them, not allowing them to get into trouble. But now that my worst fears had happened, while I wasn't mad at God, I was still believing the lie that He would just allow my life to become this endless fiasco of suffrage with no breaks. My mind battled with the Scriptures telling me that God came here so that we would have life abundantly (John. 10:10) and countering it with passages like in Romans 8:18, explaining how our present sufferings won't even compare to the amazing things that will one day be revealed to us. Or in 1 Peter 5:10, where it's written that we will have to "suffer for a little while."

These three verses, while meant to encourage, ran wild in my head, and the enemy was attempting to use them against me to do the opposite of encourage instead to bring me down in defeat. I wrestled with the fact that yes, Jesus did come for us to have abundant life, but my mind countered that while explaining that maybe that doesn't mean here; maybe it just means we will get to live life abundantly while in heaven. And that this world is just going to be a life of suffering in pain, with no good to come on earth to those who believe in Him.

The other verses seemed to back this up that we are told flat out we are going to suffer, so why was I surprised that all of this was happening around me? I tried desperately to hold tight that these tough circumstances here wouldn't matter one day once I see Jesus, face to face. But that didn't encourage me to want to live; it encouraged me to want to die and just get the pain of this world all over with and to an end already.

As a side note, yes, that previous statement seems deep and dark, with the idea of not wanting to live. That might worry some of you, and this is a huge topic on its own that we're going to dive deeply into in a chapter on mental health. But for those of you who may not understand the struggle completely with mental illness, there is a hard rope pulling from each side of the Christian battling mental illness. One side accepts that suffering is a requirement to the Fall and living life here amongst sin (which is pulling us to one side), while the other side is pulling us toward all the promises and the appealing side of death, which is no more heartbreak or pain and, instead, eternity with Christ.

I think this is why I was struggling with the Scriptures I knew and deciding what they meant in my situation. The things meant to give me hope were also waging war, and my mind was using them as ammo to gun down any possible hope floating around in my mind. But being now a year into this recovery war, God has provided tools to use as weapons that I've been able to pick up along the way, equipping me more for the rest of this war. The reality I know now is that Christ allows pain and heartache to happen. We will have to suffer for a while, and while it may seem never-ending, like things just continue to pile on and pile up on top of us, there are moments of joy and abundance He gives us. The abundant life is not meant to just be lived out in heaven, but here on earth as well. He provided this when He won the ultimate battle over death, by nailing it to a cross.

Before His death, things were dependent on what we did and how we lived. But because of His resurrection and His life, we are now free to mess up and fail as the clumsy human beings that we are. Before His death, we didn't have His presence with us, but because of His life, we now have His presence, the Holy Spirit, inside of us. Before His death, we had reason to fear the depths of hurts and pains and death, but now because of His life, we no longer need to fear death. Instead, we get to look forward to the life here on earth, getting to share His love with others, and to keep our eyes fixed ahead on life eternal spent with Him.

We can be broken and upset. The painful things of life will overtake us, and words, even if we know them to be true, will not repair things that have been completely shattered. I know that Christ is the ultimate healer, but He never promised to fix us completely from our injuries. While He can do the impossible, He did not heal us where we no longer suffer from aches and pains in our bodies. While He can restore all that is broken, and while we understand His Scriptures give us hope in life, at the same time, those verses did not put Devin's shattered leg back together perfectly, nor my broken clavicle or broken spine. However, that does not mean God is not good, because He really truly is.

The result of sin entering the world meant there was now a barrier between us and God. Now, He could have stopped this. He could have made us all machines that function perfectly, never messing up, and never allowing sin to be a thing. However, He allowed sin as a result of giving us free will. He doesn't force us to follow Him or love Him because He gave us the free choice to either walk hand in hand with Him in life, or to do our own thing and seek our desires. I think this is so beautiful; He never needed us, but He wants us so desperately so that we can experience His love. But because He loves us so much, He refused to make us forcibly love Him. He allows us to walk away and not participate in life with Him.

You might be thinking ... *Okay, so what does this all have to do with pain and suffering?* So, I'll tie this all together here. Because He wanted us to have free will, the result was sin entering the world, because we free beings were never going to be able to be perfect. So, the beautiful thing that we can see amidst the mess of pain and suffering is that it's due to the love of God giving us Himself for our own choosing. While the enemy rejoices that sin is allowed to roam this earth, we can also rejoice knowing that behind the curtain, God uses the pain and suffering as a tool to draw us closer to Him. God shows us that we can run to Him in our brokenness and look forward to the ultimate healing that we get to experience one day in His presence, when we get to enter eternity with Him.

> *He will wipe every tear from their eyes. There will be no more death or mourning or crying or pain, for the old order of things has passed away. He who was seated on the throne said, "I am making everything new!" Then he said, "Write this down, for these words are trustworthy and true. Revelation 2:4-5*

Today, September 12th, 2022 is the one-year anniversary since our pup Enya entered into the golden streets of heaven and the presence of Jesus. Saturday marked one year since our initial crash, even though it feels we've been hit every day since. Needless to say, the last few days have been full of a lot of turmoil, with learning to accept things being the way they are and some things never going back to the way they once were. Over the weekend, we visited the scene of the crash, a street we have purposefully avoided all year.

We placed a photo of Enya on the side of the street where I set her down and touched her fur for the very last time. We wrote a letter to her and placed a candle in flowers there. We wanted her remembered and noticed by those passing. She was lost as the result of a careless mistake, something that cannot be undone. And as a result, she no longer gets to do life with us, and we are no longer with her. Grief isn't something I knew before to be a part of recovery.

When people think of recovery, I think our minds go to physical therapy, painkillers, small movements, and medical equipment to guide us along the way. It doesn't, or at least my mind didn't used to, go to struggling with grieving over the life that we once knew, now never the same. And while I realize that there are movements Devin and I will never be able to do again, sports we won't be able to play, limitations we once didn't have to follow, we have been grieving the things we once were able to do. That's been one of the toughest parts of this recovery. We've had to learn to be hopeful and fix our minds on things that we hope to do again one day, while at the same time accepting the things that will damage or hurt us even more.

Walking through the grieving process of this recovery is no joke. And to anyone out there reading this that may have a similar story or journeyed through this valley of loss of movement grief, I see you, and I'm incredibly sorry for that life you had to say goodbye to.

To those who have lost someone in an incident maybe similar to ours or have had to say goodbye to a loved one who was ripped from you, without being able to actually properly say goodbye, I hear you. I see and hear the pains of your heart that ache for the life you once got to share with that special loved one, and now have to love from this side on earth while they are no longer in your arms. I understand this grief too. Now, having had to walk through both types of grief this year, and all the while attempting to learn to use our bodies all over again, it has been rough to put it lightly.

And although we cannot undo the things that have been done to us, we were able to find some ways to put some things to rest that we no longer want to wrestle with each day anymore. For example, I know people expect you to do the necessary steps to have closure in hard circumstances; I find trouble accepting that real closure will ever be completely possible. I can never put an end to my love for Enya, so my heart will still ache for her, and I can't close the door on the life I wish I still had living with her next to me.

And at the same time, I can't just close out my feelings to the hurts and physical pains Devin and I face each day now. We can't ignore the shooting pains, or the early arthritis that has suddenly been sprung on us. So full closure on those things I don't believe is possible either. But in both these scenarios, I do believe there are steps that we are, and have been, able to take to loosen the grip of pain that has entangled us this past year.

On Saturday, choosing to face the scene where we almost lost our lives was a way we wanted to pull one finger up from the grasp the enemy had as a way to inflict pain on us. Another fear of mine has been others forgetting Enya and not honoring her in the way she deserved. So that same day, I went to a tattoo shop and got a permanent mark on my arm in the hopes that others will ask about it, so I can tell the legacy of the pup who shielded my life with her own. The mark shows her name with my hand holding her paw, representing how we always held on to each other. Another finger that was pinning us down is now letting up a bit, and not having as much control.

The beginning of our recovery required a giant leg boot for Devin, a knee brace, crutches, a walker, and a wheelchair. For myself, a big back brace, a cane, a sling, and a belt that people had to tie around me to hang on to as extra support to hold me up at times. These were pieces of equipment that I thought for a long time we would never be able to live without. This equipment wasn't just essential to our everyday lives, but necessary to be able to get out of bed to use the restroom. So, as a way to crush the lies that those pieces of equipment would be permanent in our lives, Devin took his boot and knee brace and threw them in the garbage. I grabbed the belt, my sling, back brace and did the same. Another finger of the enemy's, pulled up from his grip.

We will have hard things that come upon us, but they don't have the final say or have to squish us with their grips of pain. There might be temporary necessities that pain us for a time, but we can have hope that they don't write the ending pages of the story or hold the title of the book in their grip. We can still have hope in our hopeless circumstances. Even when they might be for our foreseen lives on earth, they will not carry on into our eternal lives with Christ.

We closed our Saturday evening after many tears from the things we reflected on and the memories that held so much weight of that date; while it was a day to grieve, there was also so much to rejoice in. While the sting of death often takes front and center stages in life, I'm reminded that God still holds power over death and does not allow it to have the final say. While our accident caused so much grief, it also opened our eyes to the things that most people take for granted in everyday life.

We are still alive, when Devin and/or myself could have died, and, by the words of the first responders on scene, the crash should have taken our lives. And with the extent of our injuries, it is nothing short of a miracle that we both are able to move, walk, and run today! So while we shed tears for the pup we lost and the movements we no longer have, we also wanted to end the day by reminding others that God is our protector, and His healing hand has continued to be on us. We still get to have each other and live our lives sharing the good news of His love.

The evening was closed out by thanking Christ for saving the both of us, for allowing us to still be with family, to still get to travel, to run races, to swim in the ocean, to hike trails, and to sleep in the same bed together again. There is so much to grieve for the lives we lost that will never be again. But there is an immeasurable amount our eyes are now opened to, and reminders that this life is temporary and nothing matters here, except for loving the people around us and spreading God's love in all that we do.

This is how we wage war on the enemy—by refusing to let the things that He puts straight in our path to harm us to take control of our viewpoints on life. Those difficult things may be right in front of us, but because of the hope and guidance we have, with our eyes ultimately fixed on Christ, we can walk through that difficult thing in our path. At the same time, we can also remain thankful that we get to climb the mountain in front of us that holds the beautiful view God has given us. To end the night, I drove for the first time as a way to face fear. I saw this as taking the first step up the mountain.

I'll start closing out this chapter on this note. I heard this quote a while back that has really stuck with me. It said: *"Go laugh in the places that you've cried. Change the narrative."*[3] *- (Anonymous)*

While this isn't a Christian quote, or to my knowledge even a Christian author, I think it's something powerful that can remind us to seek the joy of Christ while in the middle of our sufferings. There are places that seem dark and painful, and the idea pops into our heads that we'll feel closer to God once things settle down, and we make it out on the other side of this mess.

But God doesn't ask us to go through the scary places of darkness alone. He asks us to hold His hand while we walk through them and look for Him working through those times. Look for His hand in the midst of the heartache. Look for His love in the middle of the pain. Look for His heart in the trouble and see the mercy He pours out on you through the suffering you're feeling. This doesn't mean that we live our lives ignoring pain or laughing in times when we should be crying. But the places of deep pain do not need to hold the tight grip on us that they do. When we acknowledge that God is working through those times, we begin to change the narrative from the enemy hurting us and shift our eyes to the God growing us. We change whose power has the ultimate hold on us when we find reasons to rejoice and have joy in the middle of the battle.

In his book *The Last Supper on the Moon*, author Levi Lusko writes this:

*"Being pruned is not punishment; it is a reward. If anyone grows fruit, the Father prunes so they can bear more fruit."*[4]

You see, the Father not only walks with us and allows us to have joy in the midst of troubling valleys, but we can rejoice knowing that we are like a branch of fruit that needs to be pruned in order to be kept up and continue to bear more fruit. I think of it like this: I felt strong in my faith and my walk with God before the accident. And maybe I felt like I was bearing fruit by pointing others to Christ by being an example of His love. And while that was great, and maybe in my eyes looked like a lot of fruit was being produced for the kingdom, the Gardner saw that my branches needed to be pruned a bit. This wasn't to punish me, but instead, it was so that more fruit could continue to grow and develop even more.

So, I want to encourage you by leaving you with this: you might be walking through something hard, and it feels like you're getting chopped in places that feel uncomfortable. Know that the Father is working. Looking back now, I think of moments that I expected we would never get out of, and our recovery would continue on in grueling pain. I remember when I didn't think that we would make it this far. But here we are now, continuing to be pruned and now growing more fruit through our story while getting to share God's miracle in our lives with others.

*"You did not choose me, but I chose you and appointed you so that you might go and bear fruit—fruit that will last..." John 15:16*

# Chapter 7: Medications & Mental Health

*"You are not your intrusive thoughts. They're kind of like weeds. Yeah, they're in the garden, but you sure as heck didn't plant them."*[1] *- @disabilityhealth*

ALRIGHT, THIS IS A huge topic. We're about to dive into the nitty gritty of it all, and things might get uncomfortable. But sit tight; I pray God can use this to teach me and you some new things about Him along the way.

In our current day and age, therapy, mental health, mental illness, antidepressants, anxiety, panic attacks, they are all becoming words more familiar in our vocabulary than ever before. We used to be in a time where most of those words were hushed and highly looked down upon by others. But now, while I believe the topic of overall mental health is being discussed more openly, I still think our generation doesn't know how to address it and has a lot to learn on truly coming alongside those of us who walk through this darkness on a daily basis.

I've titled this chapter "Medications & mental health" because even though those are two topics on their own, in my journey, they've walked hand in hand, often igniting the other and making things worse off than they would be alone. Let me explain by saying that

I am a big advocate for those who need medications in order to get through everyday life. I don't believe this is ungodly or anything to be ashamed of.

I believe that God has given us medications as tools to help mental illnesses and brains that have been devoured by anxiety, depression, PTSD, and the like. It doesn't make you any less than, or less valuable, because you take medication. It is a tool Christ has handed us to put in our toolboxes that allows some of us to build the projects of life when, without them, we'd be people staring at a nail in a piece of wood, unsure and unequipped on how to build the house in front of us.

I feel like I need to back up a bit to help you understand where I'm coming from and what I've learned along the way when addressing medications for the brain. I hope my history of both struggling to watch people I love suffer from prescription addictions, as well as going on a journey myself where I walked through many days of trial and errors with medicine can encourage someone out there who might also have a similar story, or unsure how to navigate through your own medication and mental health journey.

A little backstory...

Growing up, as I've already mentioned a bit before, I struggled with living in a home with an abusive mother. And while I miss her terribly and hate that she no longer walks this earth with me, the environment of growing up around her has really caused a lot of pain and trauma that I still am learning to walk through, even when she's not here and no longer causing pain to me.

My mom was one of the loveliest people you'd ever meet. She would always encourage us to seek out the homeless, not only to feed them but to become their friend and share about God. I specifically remember when I was little, we had a grocery store down the street from our house. My mom noticed after a while that the same homeless man was sitting outside of this market just about every time we were there. So, she began making him meals, having conversations with him, and befriending this man we came to know as John.

Now while I think most people are happy with just feeding the homeless, Mom wanted to do more with that. She told me one day that I should draw him some pictures, which I gladly did, as I was obsessed with everything art at that age. She didn't stop there—she kept thinking of the things that would actually do something to just fill John's stomach, but to make him feel more confident and valuable in himself. He had a long shaggy beard and matted hair. So Mom went into the nearby haircut salon and got John a gift card to be able to go get a haircut and wash.

I remember how broken my mom was months later, reading the newspaper and learning that a homeless man crossing the street nearby was involved in a hit and run and died. She immediately called the police department, where they confirmed that this man was our new friend John. Mom was devastated. And I share this story to show that Mom was not a monster. She had an unbelievable amount of love for others in her heart. But addictions and mental illness took over most moments of her day, and these moments of her doing big acts of love were unfortunately overshadowed by the destruction that was also caused from her.

Mom struggled with a lot of heartache in her life. From losing her dad in a traumatic way at just twelve years old to struggling with family relationships, getting divorced, and then having a traumatic miscarriage just before my birth, these things piled on her. I believe the trauma and mix of incorrect medications shaped her brain to do things that were not really her and just began to hurt her even more.

She struggled for thirty years with being on medications that were supposed to only be temporary, but after being prescribed over and over, she became addicted and reliant on things that were actually doing more harm than good to her brain and heart. These drugs diluted her mind, and I now understand that the blowups and random rages weren't random at all. She was fighting an intense war in her mind, and the dark side was winning.

Mom loved our family, but because of the side effects of extreme paranoia and anxiety, she would become obsessed and controlling over every area of our lives. As a kid, I didn't understand how I was doing everything "right" and, at the end of the day, was still getting pushed down and screamed at for what a terrible person I was. I didn't understand why I was being threatened with lies. But now as an adult, I understand completely. She loved me and my family so much, and was so incredibly terrified of losing us by us walking away, that control was the only way she could figure out in her mind to keep us what she thought was "safe."

Calling police over, going through multiple child protective service meetings: these were normal things we went through during my life. After a while, my family gave up on those resources. We were uneducated as so many in this world are with the effects of mental illness, and the forefront of our minds was how to just stop the abuse being inflicted on our family. We were blind to see that what was happening wasn't just abuse. It was an addiction, a battle my mom was suffering from, and we had no way of stopping it.

Now I give this snippet background on a good chunk of my life and the environment that I grew up in not to trash my mom. Like I said, I love and miss her so much. But because like a lot of our world today, I didn't understand the battle she was undergoing. And because I didn't comprehend it, I tried to run away from it for so long. My family grew up terrified of medications and completely against mental health drugs. We thought they were the enemy. And now as an adult, after my own experiences, I see how dangerous they can be, but also the people that they have worked for then when given correctly and the way God can change a person's life for the better through them.

I've been involved in therapy for many years, and whether you battle mental health or not, I'm a big believer that everyone needs a therapist. It is so helpful to grow and stretch ourselves through the things that have shaped us and the environments we face each day. After many years of attending therapy, I was still struggling but also growing tremendously. Because of the unsafe environment and mental, emotional, and physical abuse I encountered growing up, and sharing that in therapy for so many years, my therapist came to the conclusion that it was time to maybe consider taking medications as a new tool to take on the depression, anxiety, and PTSD I was facing each day. I've always had major sleeping issues, not just your normal run-of-the-mill "why can't I sleep" type of situation but because of being abused and threatened, especially late at night, throughout childhood. Being abused when I said I was tired and wanted to go to bed at five years old, and then having a parent turn around and tell you what a terrible child you are was confusing and traumatizing. Mom suffered from major sleep issues and often wouldn't go to bed, even after taking her sleeping medication that she was highly addicted to.

I didn't understand it at the time, but nights were where she became lonely, where the quietness haunted her and when the world began shutting down. She grew paranoid and afraid that the darkness and being alone would overtake her. Nearly every night of my growing up in that house with her meant staying up, sometimes not sleeping at all, and oftentimes being yelled at all night long.

So, when I tell someone I have sleeping problems now as an adult, and they suggest that I just drink some hot tea or take some melatonin … yeah. I actually have learned it's a much bigger issue than those things will help with. And while I was really put off on the idea for a long time, and terrified of medications after witnessing the torment and destruction in my mom's life, Devin and I heavily researched, read all the books we could, and prayed about the decision diligently before agreeing I'd try this new route out.

Now, because of the drugs my mom was on for so long, we didn't realize until late in my life that she was actually on these medications while pregnant with myself and my little sister. This turned out to be a huge reason as to why I respond poorly to anxiety medications and medications prescribed after surgeries, such as narcotics. They destroyed me and only made my situations and pain levels greater. I was always extremely paranoid and anxious, as my pain levels would increase seemingly after taking the drugs that were supposed to be helping my pain. I got to unbearable states where I would scream all night long at times in such excruciating pain. Doctors were always confused and didn't understand what was going on with me.

So, after finding this information out, I began taking the antidepressants cautiously, on top of anxiety medication as needed. After a couple of months, I wasn't noticing any changes. So, my doctor upped it, and this continued—the pattern of increasing more and more as the months went by when I was noticing no progress, other than a nauseous stomach each time the dosage changed. I was becoming frustrated, because I thought I was doing something God was guiding me toward, but it wasn't changing my brain chemistry. And although I was still working hard in therapy, the lack of sleep was catching up to me more and more.

It might make more sense to you now why I told the paramedics at the scene of the crash to not give me narcotics. Morphine was the only medication that I never had a major freak-out moment with. After dislocating my shoulder in high school and being given morphine at the emergency room, later on in life learning that it was not a narcotic, it now makes sense to me why I can handle it. But even while it doesn't give me weird side effects, it also doesn't really help me for very long. While in the hospital, and after attempting to insist on only being given morphine and avoiding narcotics for so long, the doctors and nurses explained I was at my limit for what they could give me, and the only alternative left was narcotics.

This is still a hot topic in my life that we don't fully understand, even after doing research and understanding that it's a result of my mom being addicted to narcotics, anxiety medications, and sleeping medications. We still never know how I'm going to respond when I get out of a surgery. We are always surprised by how great the pain gets and how badly it attacks my brain. And learning that things like this also affect my little sister. It's a journey we're still on the road learning about, but now you have some backstory on why I'm cautious when it comes to medications and the field of medicine.

*****

While in the hospital, after a few days of being off my antidepressant medications, they began giving me my normal dosage again with my nightly medications that consisted of about twenty different pills. After a couple days of being awake in the hospital, I was realizing that I couldn't function like my normal routine of going days on end without sleep. My body was now broken, and I wasn't healing in the ways I needed to because of my lack of rest.

I would lay in bed with extreme pain. My mind would run wild and feast on itself due to my lack of sleep. My PTSD was at the forefront of my mind, now not only because of my childhood, but also because of the crash. I would lay there reliving the crash over and over again, spiraling into darkness. Because of all of this, I finally agreed to be put on sleeping medications in order to properly heal. Now they never worked like they do and should with most people. They often knocked me out for three to four hours at a time. And while this seemed amazing to me because it was more than I ever got before, I learned this still wasn't normal, and my body was yet again fighting a medication that was meant to help me. So began the journey of new medications.

Now I'll go on a little sidebar here. I realize I'm not making a great case for medications, and in no way am I putting them down. I have heard stories and witnessed the help and relief they have helped give people and the way God has used them in people's lives for good. I share my story because while there is a lot of good that can come from them, a big part of my story is how they did cause a lot of harm in my mind.

Mental medications are tricky, because every dose is handled differently depending on each person. And because drugs work differently and aren't fully understood, it is definitely a trial-and-error game, especially when first starting out on the first doses. You might be confused to what this all has to do with our story. And on my end, it actually has taken the front stage throughout our journey of recovery.

I wasn't just dealing with recovering physically from broken bones and learning how to live life differently. On top of the childhood trauma, I was now experiencing PTSD and depression in new areas of my mind, and not only battled the things that were ingrained in my head emotionally at a young age. Now my body was holding onto the effects of trauma that happened to me, that happened to Devin, and that happened to Enya.

I've been questioned a lot and misunderstood as to how I can call myself a Christian and, at the same time, take medication for my broken brain. I was told I needed to pray harder, that I wasn't trusting God enough, and that I was living in sin with my constant state of mental instability. And I can tell you honestly that every moment of my mental health journey has brought me closer to Christ. I've gone through my deepest hurts and some of the darkest battles in my mind that only led me closer to Him, not further away.

While I don't always understand it, while I've prayed for Him to take it away, and while I hate being in a place where my mind wreaks havoc on my thoughts and heart, I don't believe I'm living in sin. At least not when I'm going up and facing it for war. In the moments that I'm giving in to worry and allowing anxiety to rule my thoughts when I'm told not to worry, I feel much guilt. I feel like a terrible Christ follower. And I do everything I can to hand those worries over to God and remember what He says in Scripture, and what He has spoken personally to me in my heart.

My college degree is in theology; this is basically the study of the Bible. And I've studied it and meditated on the Bible, cover to cover, for most of my life. But just because I know things as a matter of fact because of His Word, there are these problems in mental health that don't allow you to always line up what your mind knows and the way your body responds to that knowledge.

I have a note in my phone I wrote one day when experiencing a battle between what I knew to be true and what my bodily trauma was fueling my anxiousness with. I wrote:

*It doesn't matter if you can wrap your head around the theology logically of your circumstances. Sometimes your biology doesn't allow you to physically feel the theological peace you know full and well.*

Now let me unpack that and what I mean a bit. We can be full-send Christians, dedicated followers, servants who lays down their lives daily in all surrender to Christ. And at the very same time, our bodies that have gone through trauma and shock, while holding onto those things, doesn't communicate correctly with our thoughts. Our minds will tell us we are safe, that God is holding us and has control. However, every nerve in our bodies is in distress and in fight-or-flight mode. Something I've learned is that your body doesn't reason well with reason. I still suffer from the effects of abuse as well as our crash and the shock and trauma that came from that. And while medications didn't work out for me and allow my body to respond in ways that would calm it down and help assure it wasn't in danger, there are some things that have been helpful—they haven't cured but have made a difference along my recovery road with releasing trauma my body is holding onto and using to attack my mind.

EMDR is a type of therapy I highly recommend if you suffer from anxiety, trauma, or major phobias in your life. I've gone through years of this kind of therapy, working through many different issues my body was holding onto. It sounds like some voodoo or made-up process, but it's highly effective; and as a skeptic of most things in life, I can say that this can be extremely helpful when worked through diligently.

If you aren't familiar with EMDR, it is defined by the EMDR Institue, Inc. as: "(Eye Movement Desensitization and Reprocessing) is a psychotherapy that enables people to heal from the symptoms and emotional distress that are the result of disturbing life experience" [2] And while I don't understand it all completely, I can say that I highly recommend it if you're suffering from your body controlling your mind and being unable to release trauma caused by instances from your past. This hasn't by any means cured me, but I do recommend it because although the medication route wasn't helpful to me, EMDR is a tool that has been helpful in my healing journey.

After all of this, and now sharing a bit of my own road with walking through mental health wars and medication trial and error, I will say that I'm still on this recovery road. I have really dark and terrible days in my mind, and my brain often takes over and tries to rule over God speaking to me that He is with me.

I've opened up and shared my story in this area with others, and while oftentimes it is highly misunderstood, I do want to bring to light the importance of learning about mental diseases to help those you love as they navigate this possible life-long battle in front of them. It gets really lonely and exhausting. It's draining to fight a war and then to come out on the other side for a breather, seeking help and comfort to only be met with shame. It's heartbreaking to be misunderstood and left after sharing and being vulnerable with others. It increases the power of the mental games that are played when often our biggest lie in our heads is how unworthy and invaluable we are due to our mental illness; and to have others walk away and step out of the picture only confirms those lies as truth in our heads.

So I plead with you, stick with those who are on the battlefield right now. Stay with them through the darkest moments, and remind them that there is joy despite the battle going on inside of them. You can wage war with them when you take a swing at those lies of them feeling less than; and when you stand by them to fight, one by one, the lies start coming down, and the sunlight peaks through the clouds on the battlefield, even if just for a moment. Sometimes a moment makes all the difference for someone who has been fighting a war for years on end.

There is this movement going around online and social media accounts where the hashtag "postyourpill" came to my attention. The idea behind this movement is to share your personal story with the pills that you take in your mental health journey, and to end the stigma that mental health isn't as big of a deal as it truly is. After years of keeping this side of my story a secret, and only confiding in a couple of people in my life, I felt that God was stirring in my heart that He wanted me to share and be vulnerable in my mental health battle.

Shortly after going off of all the medications I was on just six months or so into recovery, we made this decision when my mental health was only growing worse, suicidal thoughts were more often, and when there was honestly no good results we were seeing. I was suffering not only from the mind games, but the drugs intended to help me sleep were actually causing me to stay awake more. My mind was spiraling more often now that my waking hours were constant, and even my normal naps, where I often would get the most sleep in a day, were becoming far and in between.

And after being on so many medications not only for the recovery of my broken bones, but also the side effects of the mental medications I was on, they were causing me to gain weight at a rapid speed. Within a short period of time, I had gained over thirty pounds, and with not being able to move physically the ways I used to, my health became a concern. I felt terrible about myself and having never struggled with weight issues in my past before, I was developing eating disorder problems and obsessing over the way I looked. My mind that already attacked me daily was just given a whole other reason to call myself unworthy and look down on myself in guilt and shame for the way I now looked.

After the negative effects piled up and finally reached their limit, and we decided it was best to stop playing the lab rat who was being switched from medication to medication every few days. Instead, we focused on coming off of those pills and going back to square one on facing these battles without these tools, searching for new ways to wage war on the attacks in my mind. After going off these medications, I decided to lean into what Christ was stirring in my heart and share my story with others about the road of mental health problems I was facing and the medication journey I had been on. I was terrified; sharing this kind of thing with anyone is scary, let alone sharing on social media where anyone can see it shakes your bones. But I followed Christ and took the step I believe He was asking me to take. And so, I wrote the post with the hashtag #postyourpill. Here's the post I shared online:

*#postyourpill*

*I don't want to post this; however, I think God can use my fears & insecurities for His good & perfect purpose. My hopes are to encourage someone else out there who may be battling something similar.*

*If that's you, I'm so sorry & want to be here for you. Reach out any time & I will fight the battle alongside you. Battles can't be won alone; they need an army. Please consider recruiting me to support you along the way.*

*I've shared a few thoughts on mental health before, but I've never been this open before. Not many people know this part of my story, but I really hope it helps someone out there & that I can see God work through it in the lives of others.*

*Let me start by saying medication was never on my front lines; it was my last line of defense.*

*I witnessed the people I love throughout my life struggle & battle the effects of addiction, bad side effects, or* misdiagnoses of medication. I believed medication was the enemy & to run in the opposite direction of it.

The phrases "oh the coffee gives me anxiety!" or "I'm depressed because I'm not getting XY or Z in life" or "that *fill in the blank joke* is giving me PTSD" are words that aren't taken lightly. Please consider rephrasing your situational anxiousness and sadness, because for those who truly struggle with these mind battles; it isn't something we joke about.

And while we appreciate your input, the advice to "cure us" does not work by drinking more water, cutting out media before bed, eating a balanced diet, or "choosing joy" if you're a *real* Christian. The phrase "choose joy" is not a Bible verse. I love my God with all that I am, but that doesn't fix the disease I have in my mind.

I've picked up every Christian book & Bible study I could find on this subject. I've dug into the depths of the Bible, searching for the healing my heart & mind so desperately desires.

But I'm still not cured. I'm also no less sure that my God reigns and lives inside me.

I don't doubt for a second that He died for me; that He pictured my face on the cross. And I don't believe He enjoys watching His daughter hurt & feel the pains of this world.

*I know He allows suffering, and He doesn't always stop troubles from tripping me as I walk down the road of life. He allows it, so He can use it.*

*And when I think of the biggest moments I've suffered in my life, I see Christ and how deeply my love for Him grew. I feel the soreness of how my faith was stretched & turned into muscular faith in the end.*

*For a long time, I believed the lie of the enemy that taking medication made me a faithless Christian, that my belief in God wasn't "strong enough," and I often confused the allowing of suffering to be mixed up with God making me miserable on purpose here, and the only relief I'd get would be in heaven someday. That didn't make me want to live, and it weighed me down so much mentally that I physically couldn't do the work of God and love others the right way.*

*I used Scripture, multiple kinds of therapies, and any advice I could get to go to war against my disease. Unfortunately, nothing beat it. It continued to cut me down.*

*The relief I saw on my therapist's face the day I considered medication after years of struggling; I'll never forget.*

*This isn't a new battle for me that came on recently. It didn't happen overnight after I lost people I love. And, although you might be thinking it, it wasn't caused because of our car crash a few months ago. Although, our car accident definitely amplified a lot of my triggers.*

*It's been an enemy I've been at war with since at least junior high; it's grown as trauma, abuse, & grief have occurred, and that definitely made it stronger none the less.*

*I know what it's like to not want to wake up. I also know what it's like to love Jesus wholeheartedly while struggling with that thought.*

*It makes sense to me to want to get away from the sickness & suffering in this world and to just be by the side of Christ already. And although I believe God doesn't condemn those who have fallen in this battle, I do push on because I know His will is to live and not take my life on my own timetable.*

*So here we go...*

*I'm opening up this door because I believe it's something God wants me to do in this moment. I don't have all the answers, and I'm still fighting this battle like so many out there.*

*I've felt like a lab rat lately. The amount of medication attempts + fails with prescriptions ... I've lost track of. I don't like putting ingredients in my body that could hurt what I believe is the temple of the Holy Spirit. So, I make sure each prescription is deeply researched by my own team, which includes my therapist, psychiatrist, and husband.*

*I get what it's like to have careless doctors throw medication in your face & not follow up with you. Or not bother to look at your chart and be prescribed something that hurts my health in other areas.*

*Medications have landed me in the ER with side effects that just add to the already difficult war. The journey is a mountain & I understand the heavy weight of the backpack full of guilt, pain, and endless emotions.*

*I know what a gift it is to feel and love deeply, but I also know how much harder that makes this journey when medications twist up feelings or even make you numb from having any.*

*I get what it's like to want to give up.*

*But I'm posting this because I want you to try again with me.*

*I know what hopelessness feels like; I carry that burden too. But I know that God is here now. He's doing this climb with us. He's asking us to hope just a little more for that beauty we'll see at the peak of this climb.*

*I'm here fighting for and with you.*

*Let's #hopesomemore.*

*Joy isn't a feeling we choose but choosing defiance in the middle of the storm. To keep pushing through & hope even the slightest is what the joy of Christ truly is.*

*So here I am in my most raw form.*

*Hi, my name is Jo, and I battle:*

*PTSD, anxiety, depression, severe insomnia.*

*For the last month, I've taken a break from medications because the side effects were causing me more harm than good in my body. For a while there, I swallowed double digits of pills a day to help gear me up for the battle of my mind.*

*I don't know if I'll go back on medications any time soon. Unfortunately, I wasn't able to stand the side effect of weight gain when I wasn't noticing any help to my already messy mind games. Adding an eating disorder to the mix was not something I felt like God wanted me to mix in.*

*But I'm sharing this bit of my story to fight against the stigma against medication and that people are perfect out there. Mental illness is just as real as any other deadly body disease, and it needs treatment all the same.*

*On my medication journey, I took the pills not to cure me or fight the whole battle for me, but to help shoot some arrows at the enemy to lessen the attacks. EMDR and other forms of counseling/therapy are other warriors that act on my behalf as well, swinging swords & taking the enemy down, one trauma at a time.*

*You may believe I'm crazy, but I just call it a broken brain. And it's no different from other bones I've broken or injuries I've been through.*

*Medication is sometimes necessary in healing broken limbs, and it doesn't have to last forever.*

*I pray mine doesn't.*

*But even still, if it does ... my God is still good in the midst of the storm.*

*He's fighting for us.*

*I believe in you. He believes in you. Let's keep fighting to do the work He calls us to & continue to live to love others.*

*When all is said and done, I know God loves me. I know hard things are allowed by Him to work for my good. His perspective may be unfathomable to me, but I place my trust in Him.*

*Honestly, the "good work" really sucks right now.*

*I'm just really exhausted from this all.*

*I've been through the Bible cover to cover. I don't doubt Christ loves me & cares about me. No matter what I look like or bring to the table.*

*I understand this world is a cruddy place. That people & places mess it up with sin hurts that are just so backward. My expectations aren't for the world to get better. I know it won't until God comes & creates the new heaven and new earth. So, I don't think we should expect things to get all the way better.*

*But on the days that we can get out of bed, that we can exercise, that we can love someone, days we can share Him with others—that's what we're here for and that's a win.*

*Some days will feel like an endless battle with our minds, and I don't think sleeping and crying endlessly in those times is a sin. I think those are the days we run to our God and allow Him to hold us. When we're recharged in Him, we can then allow Him to gear us up for battle once again and fight our minds.*

*I'm here alongside you on these front lines ... and so is our God.*

*Let's go to war together.*

*#noshameinmymedgame*

I hope this encourages and gives someone else hope out there on a similar battlefield. I don't have all the answers, but I am here fighting this war alongside of you. I pray one day we get results and answers that will better help us navigate through mental health. But for today, be with those who are struggling, and if it's you who is the one growing wearing in this struggle, I'm praying for you and that God gives you some hope in this storm today. I'll close out this chapter with a few verses I find helpful, encouraging, and convicting when it comes to all we have just discussed:

"Be happy with those who are happy, and weep with those who weep." Romans 12:15

One way I have felt the most support in this journey is simply when I have someone sit beside me and cry with me. We don't need someone to have all the answers; sometimes just knowing there is someone willing to listen and hold the sword in the battle for a moment can be more helpful than you might think.

"Remember how the LORD your God led you all the way in the wilderness these forty years, to humble and test you in order to know what was in your heart, whether or not you would keep his commands." Deuteronomy 8:2

Author Kayla Stoecklein shares a great viewpoint on this verse in her book *Fear Gone Wild*. She writes:

> In the Bible, the word "wilderness" appears more than three hundred times. God's people were constantly in the wilderness, driven there either by flight or fight. In flight mode, they ran away from their circumstances, from the only home they knew, searching for safe haven. In fight mode, they wrestled with life, with God, and with their desert surroundings...

> *The wilderness has a beautiful way of prying open our hearts. As we wander through the wide-open spaces, we discover who we really are and how great our need for God really is. The wilderness isn't optional; it's an integral part of life.* [3]

I found this quote encouraging and want to challenge you to dive deep and take advantage of the desert and wilderness you find yourself in, especially in the mental health arena. Though it's a struggle, and we don't want to stay in it forever, in those moments where we are stranded there, keep an eye out for what God is teaching you in the midst of it. Those lessons learned in the wilderness shape our faith and grow us deep in relying on Him in new ways. The wilderness is not a waste.

"And the God of all grace, who called you to his eternal glory in Christ, after you have suffered a little while, will himself restore you and make you strong, firm and steadfast." 1 Peter 5:10

This suffering may seem unending, and maybe it will go on for our entire lives here on earth. But I have to hold onto the hope that the trials are growing my faith, and my faith is what I get to carry on into eternity. It's shaping who I am and, more importantly, how I view God and what I believe about Him.

I'll end on this last thought. I know what it's like to not want to be on earth anymore, and as I've shared, I know of the eternity that awaits those who believe in Him—no more suffering or pain. A perfect heaven with a perfect God holding me will be what I come face to face with someday. But in the meantime, what if these really difficult things that I'm dealing with are teaching me a better understanding of what it means to grow in faith and ultimately become more like

Him? If this is the reason for suffering, then I can have hope that it is for my good, and a part of His good and perfect road for my life.

*"And we know that in all things God works for the good of those who love him, who have been called according to his purpose." Romans 8:28*

# Chapter 8: Sitting Still

*"Be still, and know that I am God; I will be exalted among the nations, I will be exalted in the earth." Psalm 46:10*

I'M NOTORIOUS FOR NOT sitting still. Well, I used to be anyway. Rewind to every day before our car accident and you'd find me with one excuse after another on reasons not to sit down, unable to sit still, and, quite frankly, not understanding what it means to take a breath. Part of this might be the way life was growing up in a house of always being on the go— my three siblings and I were heavily involved in multiple softball and baseball teams each. And as much as I love that part of my life, I do think it plays a factor in why I tick the way I do today.

My family hardly ever slept. Call it anxiousness, or just no time to actually do so, but we were pretty much known for having giant softball tournaments with three to five games a day and playing those games with an hour or two of sleep if we were lucky. After every game, each play was deeply analyzed, whether good or bad. Most of the time things would get heated, voices would be raised, doors slammed, tears shed. But we'd start back over the next day and go through this cycle every tournament, and most practices in between.

But because of those late nights and persevering through over 100-degree weather, no sleep, and anxiety at all-time highs, I think this is a blessing and a curse that was wired into me. In some senses, I hate it because I've never found true, restful sleep. The words "winding down" after a long day are foreign to me. I keep going, often to a fault, one thing to the next. This was the pattern of my life.

As I got into my adult life, the weight and exhaustion of a no sleep schedule, and even when I would sleep, I would never feel rested, never rejuvenated for the next day's activities. Burnt out was an understatement as I got into my third year of college, struggling to juggle multiple jobs on top of full-time classes and being heavily involved in volunteering in a variety of areas of our church. I was also attempting to balance relationships with friends and family in between.

The first semester I transferred from community college and entered into Bible college to finish out my degree, my body was done. It had been running on low oil, low fuel, and with all the dashboard lights telling me "Warning!" for far too long. My first week in my dorm room, I became extremely sick. I ended up missing most of my classes and having to constantly play catch-up, as I struggled with being in and out of the hospital and doctors' appointments because my body was growing so sick. So yeah, you could say I'm pretty good at not sitting still.

And while all of that really drained me and hit me hard, I continued to fight against my body and God telling me I needed to slow down and, throughout the years, found new ways to push my body to its limits. Working multiple jobs, still not knowing how to sleep properly, juggling taking care of those I love, and everything in between. I think because of the way I grew up, it was ingrained in me to keep pushing, keep going, and when your body is at its limits, tell it to keep going. This was the softball field mantra, and it crept into every area of my life.

Just before our car accident last year, I was working three different nanny jobs, on top of volunteering in multiple areas of church and running my own photography business. Now if you think that doesn't sound so bad, just know I agree with you. So, it didn't seem so bad when I was also working on my dad's old house to prepare to sell it, constantly bandaging up things that were breaking, and when I couldn't fix it, trying to track down a handyman who could. In the middle of trying to sell that house, we were also continuing our search for our own home. In the midst of that, Enya was in and out of the vet for treatments, or checkups, and even in between her appointments, I was dreading and anticipating her next one with the fears of uncertainties and bad news that might come with it.

Less than two years before this time, all my siblings had moved out to the Midwest, and nearly every day we were trying to plan our next visit to see them, as the distance was growing heavily on our hearts. While our hearts and minds were in the Midwest, we were attempting to juggle being present here with the family that remained within minutes of us, always looking for the next opportunity to spend time growing with them. And if it wasn't family, it was planning on the next get-together with friends and doing our best to grow relationships deeply with being fully committed to every activity thrown our way.

So, after this pattern continued on, and my stubborn heart refused to take God's invitation to rest after all those years, it literally took Him throwing on the brakes in my life to get me to sit still. I think the people surrounding our circumstances thought this was a blessing in disguise and finally a way to get me to rest. But let me tell you ... things were not that simple. I grew to hate every single day that I couldn't move, couldn't accomplish a task, couldn't keep my eyes open when fighting my darnedest to beat the medication drowsiness. I was being forced to sit still and let God be God, and what I realized was that my sitting still was not only a problem due to not accepting God's invitation to rest in Him, it had also become an idol and a control issue in my life.

When I refused to let go of things after I had done everything in my power to fix the situation, when I had put in all the hours needed for work, when I poured everything and more into the relationships around me but still felt like I needed to do more so people would love me: in all of these situations, I was pushing my body and mind past the limits that God had created for me as a way to warn that I needed to take a break and hand the controls over to Him. Every time I kept going when He told me to sit down, I was essentially telling Him that I knew better and didn't trust Him enough to take over the situation and get the results that I wanted.

A few months into recovery, I started noticing that I was still fighting this and wanting to pursue my "normal" of moving and controlling my life. It was a hard pill to swallow (which says a lot when I was taking twenty plus pills a day) when I found out ... and get this ... when you break your back, have major spinal surgery, and your body goes through serious trauma, you can't do much of anything anymore. I know, it was a shock to me too!

I began seeing how much of my identity I put into being and looking productive and a hard worker to those around me was controlling and driving my thoughts and actions. So when this identity was stripped away, and Christ was pushing me to grow in this area, I started trying to listen in on what He was trying to tell me for so many years now.

About four months into recovering, I was beginning to pursue and try to lean into what He was teaching me. It's still something I struggle with to this day, don't get me wrong. Especially now that I can move a lot better and can actually go running again. This tempts me to grab back the reins from Him. But I often remember the lessons He was teaching me throughout those first few months and try to embrace those more than I ever did before.

This was a post I wrote a few months after our accident on my social media account, and it's served as a great reminder to keep me in check and hold me accountable to the things He taught me, so that I don't fall back into temptation of pushing myself without His rest again. I don't ever want that to be a normal pattern in my life again. Here's what I wrote in my post:

> *"He makes us wait. He keeps us on purpose in the dark.*
>
> *He makes us walk when we want to run, sit still when we want to walk, For he has things to do in our souls that we are not interested in."*[1] -- Elizabeth Elliot
>
> *I'm no good at this. But now somehow, I have to be.*
>
> *I want to go running.*
>
> *I dream of backpacking, hiking, and hanging out under giant waterfalls that my God has made.*

This chapter snuck its way into the story I was writing for my life, and it turns out its rambling on a lot longer than I'd like.

But maybe this chapter makes and shapes the book.

No, scratch that; the real author of the story of my life is the one shaping it. He had this moment ready in a draft, and it was time to put it on the page.

I feel it was abrupt, but maybe that's a good reminder that I'm not supposed to be in control.

I've never been someone to sit still.

I don't allow it being productive and doing things for the kingdom of God is always at the forefront of my mind.

Never saying no.

Never wanting to miss an opportunity to love a soul.

He kept telling me to be still; I didn't know what that meant and felt guilty as if I was failing God.

I tried to sit; my body wouldn't allow it.

Go. Go ... go ... do... go... repeat.

I guess it took God literally throwing the brakes on to get me to stop.

*My body doesn't feel me. I feel broken. I don't know how to move in this body that feels foreign. And maybe that's okay though ... I shouldn't be getting too comfy here anyway, right? I mean God's already got me a sweet, cozy spot saved next to Him, so maybe it's alright that life feels floopy and uncertain.*

*Maybe God only wants His daughter to rest & heal.*

*Maybe my only job right now is to learn how to do things again.*

*To be okay on the days when I physically cannot get up from bed.*

*To not fear that the world is on my shoulders ... honestly, that's pretty prideful to think so much rests on me, huh?...*

*And maybe right now the most godly thing I can do is finally listen to Him & rest.*

*I hope I can run again someday. But for now, I'm being called to sit.*

*This journey is a trip ... but man, God, You're sure teaching me a lot of crazy cool stuff along the way.*

It's currently September as I write this. But as someone who lives in sunny Southern California, it doesn't feel like fall like other states might at this point in the year. While most other states are beginning to see the leaves change colors, and the wind getting chillier, our part of the state is threatened by multiple wildfires, an intense heatwave, and sunscreen seems necessary just to step outside for a second.

A few months ago, at the beginning of summer, my spinal doctor gave me the go-ahead that I could start trying to run again. After months of sitting still, and struggling with my body feeling cramped up, I was excited to finally, hopefully feel a little more normal and begin adding some healthier regimens into my recovery. Up until that point, I was severely struggling with my weight. After being a lab rat for so many months, on top of all the trauma my body went through and no longer being able to move much, I gained over thirty pounds during the first half of recovery.

I had never weighed that much in my life, and not only was I uncomfortable in the new body with the new hardware holding it together, but my skin didn't feel like my own. I felt the constant state of puffiness taking center stage in my everyday life. Being an athlete all my life and never sitting still, weight was never something I really had to worry about. Sure, there were a lot of moments throughout life where I wish I had that skinny dancer body that all my friends had. But it didn't rule my thoughts for very long. I always came to accept that my doctors were happy with my weight and telling me I was healthy. I was always moving and extremely active.

So now, fast forward to not being allowed to move and medications ruling my system. Not only was I struggling with the pain and heartache of the recovery process, but now a new hurdle was being thrown in my path. My mind was fatigued from everything else going on in front of me that the weight gain quickly became a stumbling block in my life. It's a year later, and I've just hit the halfway mark on my weight goals by losing sixteen of the thirty-one pounds that I gained.

I've struggled with my body image and grieved over my favorite clothes that I was able to wear for years, suddenly not fitting me anymore. I battled crash diets and exercised on a spin bike (my only allowed activity in recovery) for an unhealthy number of miles in a day, all while hardly eating, if at all some days. And even after all of that, the scale refused to budge. Guilt crept in. I didn't want to leave the house because of how ashamed I was of this new skin I was living in. It didn't seem to matter how healthy I ate, what diet pills I took, or how much I worked out. I was stuck to say the least.

I read this quote recently:

*"I keep putting things in the microwave, and God keeps putting them back in the crockpot. Whatever is distracting you today, give it a little more time."*[2] *- Bob Goff*

I want to hit more on the subject of my new battle of the year with the topic of weight and all the struggles that have come with that. Going through a major car accident didn't ever seem like it would take over my life, but battling an eating disorder and body hatred while recovering from that accident at the same time was just a double whammy. I know body image is a huge topic in itself, so I don't want that to be overlooked here. However, I'm touching on it a bit here because I think it relates a bit when it comes to the subject of sitting still as well.

Throughout this journey of learning to accept the way that I look, while also treating my body as a temple of God, almost feels like an oxymoron in itself. So, there's places throughout Scripture where

I'm told I'm beautiful, a masterpiece even in God's sight, but at the same time, I'm a temple of His Spirit and I need to make sure that I'm not damaging that temple or putting it in harm's way. You can see my confusion when in one instance I'm being told I am perfect the way I am, and the next I think I'm being told that I'm not good enough because my temple is not healthy.

After struggling with all the diets, the frustration with the scale determining my worth, and the body image idea that now consumed me, God started teaching me in the midst of it. And I hope that this is helpful to someone else who might be facing a similar battle of image. I don't mean to say I've mastered this topic. In fact, just this morning I hit a low again with my worth when I stepped on the scale after attempting the keto diet once again the last few days. The numbers hadn't changed, even after all my efforts battling grumbling stomach pains, pushing my body at the gym, and eating seemingly healthy foods. My frustration and worth were deflated yet again.

My husband went to war on my behalf when I was defeated in this area of battle once again. He reminded me that I'm in a war and this is an attack from the enemy, who is a liar, a tactic to hurt me and throw me off course. It's a way to fix my eyes on the temporary circumstances that are right in front of me, the mountain that I stand at the base of, which seems slippery and muddy, and honestly don't want to climb right now. And while the scale may be the same as it was before all my hard efforts, that doesn't determine my worth or take away from all of the victories that God has already been doing in and through our lives and our recovery this year. The enemy wants to steal my eyes away from all the good and impossible situations God has already helped us overcome. Instead, it tells me that this battle with my weight gain is not only impossible but what a failure I am that even in my best attempts, I still don't look or feel the way I once did before all of this.

As author Bob Goff mentioned in his quote shown before, he used the word "distracting." I think that's exactly what the enemy is doing to me here. He's distracting me from all the good and the areas where I can and will have victory, instead blasting the word "failure" up in bright lights where I feel everyone can see. All I want to do is curl into a ball and cry, hiding away from the world.

If the enemy can distract me and pull me into the depths of darkness in my self-worth, then he has won. He's distracting me with the way I look, instead of encouraging me to focus on the people and the things God has put in front of me to love and do for His name's sake. When I get caught up in the lies of the enemy telling me I'm a failure, I dwell and spiral. I refuse to sit still and take the rest God is telling me to take. Instead, I try to work harder, run further, and eat less but get hungry more. My stomach tells me I'm starving, while the enemy tells me I'm not worthy of food. Meanwhile, God is sitting on the sidelines, admiring this "masterpiece" He has created in me and wondering why I'm picking it apart instead of embracing it and taking it out into the world to use for His good and perfect works!

So, here's what I know to be true. Ephesians 2:10 puts it like this:

*"For we are God's masterpiece. He has created us anew in Christ Jesus, so we can do the good things he planned for us long ago."*

And while I know that I am perfect in His sight, that doesn't give me an excuse to not treat my body with the love and respect it needs to glorify Him. First Corinthians 6:19 says this:

*"Do you not know that your bodies are temples of the Holy Spirit, who is in you, whom you have received from God? You are not your own."*

So, with these two verses, here's what I think God is asking of us. That in one sense, we are a masterpiece He has created. We aren't beautiful or worth anything on our own, and we didn't do anything to get here. He has good things planned for us to do, and He has designed us perfectly for those good works. But while He loves us just the way we are, He loves us too much to have us stay that way. So, while He says He loves us, He also wants us to care for the masterpiece He has given us so that we are good hosts to the Holy Spirit that is dwelling inside of us.

The way I've learned to see it is that my God loves me and calls me beautiful. My husband loves me and tells me I'm perfect. But if a doctor were to see my weight right now, they'd tell me it wasn't good for my health. So, I think the balance needs to be made in all of this that our goals and mindset needs to be on filling our bodies with the proper nutrients God has given us, fueling it with foods that allow us to have energy and keep going in the lives He's calling us to love. But at the same time, this doesn't need to become an obsession. Our focus shouldn't be so much on our bodily images that we lose sight of those we should be serving and loving around us, becoming so fixated on how we look that we don't get to do the kingdom work we are called to do.

If we are filling our bodies with the right things, taking care of it through daily movement and exercise, and asking God to care for it, then our work is done. We have taken care of it in the ways and with the tools that He has given us. And if results aren't seen, maybe clothes still don't fit right, maybe the scale doesn't budge, and we are left still feeling insecure and unsure with why we can't look a certain way, I think we have to turn back to remembering we are His. God will take care of us, and if we have done everything we can, then the results aren't up to us. We don't have that control, and we have to believe that the answer He is giving us at the end of all our hard work is still "wait" or "be still." We have to know He is working it for our good and His perfect, purposeful plan for our lives, even if we can't see the whole picture.

Part of sitting still keeps teaching me how out of control of my circumstances I really am, having to accept and trust the One who actually does control it all. Morgan Harper Nichols puts it this way:

*"Perhaps 'keep going' does not have to mean 'keep running.' Perhaps to simply keep breathing is a miraculous feat all on its own ... especially right now."* [3]

I love that. Perhaps instead of putting myself down for how much I have failed or feeling defeated with how much further I have left to go, I can keep going by simply breathing. Recovery doesn't mean I have to keep trying to learn to run when all I'm supposed to be doing is learning how to walk again. And when I'm supposed to be sitting still, breathing and just focusing on taking the next breath are victories all on their own.

There is this verse in Exodus 14:14 where it reads:

*"The Lord will fight for you; you need only to be still."*

The Lord was telling the people that they didn't need to fight. Their only job was to rely on Him and trust Him. And this is something so crucial to the Christian life today. We will continue to face struggles, go to battle with the enemy, fight fights that we may lose over and over again, and get defeated when we feel all hope is lost.

But even though we are told to stand firm, part of that means standing firm on the ground that Christ has control of.

Standing firm doesn't mean we contain all the control or have any say in the outcome. But it means we fight in the areas He tells us to with the tools He has given us. And when we are weary, when we've done our part, it means that it is time to sit down and get bandaged up and rest for the next wave. That's where He tells us that we need to be still and rest in His Word. Continuing to fight when we have no strength left does nothing but more damage to ourselves instead of the enemy.

So maybe you're like me. This sitting still concept is foreign and pretty difficult to accept. You don't have to master it today, but I encourage you to **pray** and seek God's voice in the midst of your busyness and weariness. Don't wait and put off the rest to the point where He has to forcefully make you come to a stop and rest. It's always easier if we simply obey immediately and take His commands seriously from the start. He is fighting for us. Whether in the job atmosphere that is wearing you out, the relationships dragging you down, the financial struggles that seem overwhelming, the disease that seems never-ending, the goals that are always just out of reach, the rest that just never seems to be enough: in all these circumstances, He is fighting for you, He's fighting for me. Do your part with what He has called you to do, and only that. And then, sit. Be still. And you know how the verse goes: "know that HE is God," not you.

# Chapter 9: Loneliness

*"I WILL NEVER [under any circumstances] DESERT YOU [nor give you up nor leave you without support, nor will I in any degree leave you helpless], NOR WILL I FORSAKE or LET YOU DOWN or RELAX MY HOLD ON YOU [assuredly not]!" (Hebrews 13:5 Amplified)*

A COUPLE OF WEEKS after being released home from rehab, I assumed at this point we would begin the process of resting. But honestly the first few weeks at home were some of the most chaotic. Nearly every day, either Devin or I had a doctor appointment, X-rays, meetings with lawyers, phone appointments, you name it. Our injuries were feeling like they controlled our lives, and it was becoming quite exhausting.

Part of the agreement of being released from rehabilitation was that my psychologist, who I was seeing daily, wanted me to see a psychiatrist. She wanted this so I wouldn't have to try to navigate medications on my own anymore. This was very different from before, as I've mentioned I had tried many medications and never saw a positive result from them.

I had a video call appointment with some random psychiatrist through my healthcare plan and after finding out he was actually a child psychiatrist, this made me more comfortable actually. I felt that he must have to take a lot of precautions with diagnosing and handling medications for younger people. We sorted through all the medications that I had tried and failed on, and then after gathering all the information, he prescribed me a medication that would hopefully help with my depression and anxiety, but the big goal was for it to target my PTSD. Before ending the appointment, I asked him, like I do with every doctor before taking any medication, what the side effects would be from this. He jokingly said that the worst side effect I would have would be "getting really good sleep." He meant this to be funny, since we went over the fact that I do not really sleep. I was relieved and hopeful to know that a medication was out there that would hopefully begin to help me with this battle I was facing, decreasing some of the intensities of the war my mind was going through.

We went and picked up my medication that evening. I took it before trying to go to bed as prescribed. I proceeded to be more awake those next several hours than I had been in weeks. I was bummed, not only because it wasn't helping me with sleep, but I also wasn't noticing any response to my other symptoms in my mind. After a few hours, I was finally tired enough from my other medications that I fell asleep.

The next thing I remember was sitting on the toilet and my husband trying to keep my eyes focused on him. My ears were ringing, my eyes were blurry, and a hint of tunnel vision was affecting them. Devin was trying to ask me something. After a few moments, I realized he was trying to ask if I was okay. Devin, who was hurt himself, later described to me that in the middle of the night, he heard me moaning from the bathroom. He got in his wheelchair, with his broken leg and all his gear, and rushed to our bathroom to find me passed out and about to fall over on the toilet. Thankfully, he was there to catch me or my broken back would've not been in good shape after taking a fall like that.

The next bit is fuzzy, but I do remember he helped me get back into bed somehow, but I kept saying I didn't feel good. We began realizing that I was having a terrible reaction to the new medication I was on. It was causing me to black out, feel nauseous, and extremely high. The next few hours I remember lying in bed miserable and Devin trying to sooth and calm me with soft words as the medication was causing me to panic. When I finally felt like I was waking up a little bit, I told him I needed to try to walk to the restroom. I remember not feeling well, as Devin and my mother-in-law stood nearby, ready to help me if needed. I got to the toilet, and when I got up to wash my hands, I recall yelling, "I don't feel good." The next moment, I passed out with my mother-in-law holding me up. She called Devin to dial for an ambulance, and we began to realize the struggle I was already having with my blood pressure since the accident, now this new medication was causing my blood pressure to drop a significant amount and to reach dangerous levels.

I remember screaming, "I don't want to go back!" over and over as I began crying. I was absolutely terrified now of going back to the hospital. I knew that it would help me, but I was so defeated, knowing I had just finally gotten back home with Devin and was scared I would get stuck back in a hospital room once again and apart from him. After a few minutes, the paramedics arrived and took my blood pressure. Now seeing for themselves it was so low, they told me I needed to go into the emergency room. I begged them not to take me. They said they couldn't force me, but I really needed to be seen by a doctor. Through the tears, I agreed and spent the rest of the day in the emergency room, surrounded by doctors and nurses just as confused as I was as to why I was prescribed a medication that the number one side effect was blood pressure dropping.

Spoiler, I'm fine now. I got out of the hospital that evening and obviously never took that medication again. And while we've already touched on the whole uphill battle of medication in my life, that isn't the whole focus on this chapter. Really, the big take-away of that whole ordeal of that day going back to the hospital was how afraid I was of being alone. I think this began right after I crash; I grabbed one of the paramedic's hands on the helicopter as they airlifted me to the ER. I wanted all my visitors, no matter how tired or drugged I was in my room. Heck, half the time that I had visitors, I'm pretty sure I was sleeping, but I just wanted to know that someone was in the room with me.

Maybe this is a normal response after a traumatic incident. I know it was abnormal for me from the get-go, because although I love loving God's people, I'm also very much an introvert and need time alone in order to recover and reset my mind. So, when I was constantly asking for more people to visit in the ICU, constantly on FaceTime in rehabilitation, and eagerly anticipating seeing people who would visit and bring us meals and sit with us during our recovery, there was something about these visits that helped with feeling a little less alone in this great, big circumstance we were facing.

I remember putting out multiple posts on social media throughout our time in the hospital and during recovery. Devin and I were constantly overwhelmed by the love we felt from the amount of people reaching out to us through messages and visiting in the hospital.

We appreciated the people praying from near and far, the people who donated toward our medical expenses, and those who brought us meals throughout those first couple of months of being home. And although we felt like we were so loved and important to not only people we regularly saw but now people who we hadn't seen in years now posting about our story online, as time went on, the visits and messages became fewer and fewer.

Unfortunately, something that you can't really be prepared for is when you have to start doing the recovery process alone. There have been some overwhelmingly intense months that Devin and I have faced of feeling utterly alone. We began realizing that it was easy for people to reach out when our crash was on headline news articles. However, it started dawning on us that the people who had shared our story on social media, which we were so surprised by after not having much contact with them for so many years, weren't so much sharing for us, but were being shared as a way to be a part of the drama as it played out. We had so many people surrounding us, telling others how close they were to us and what great friends we were. And although that meant so much to us in the hospital, it was proven not true when the article was shared when we were hanging on for life in the ICU, never actually hearing from those same people when we were beginning to heal and on the road to recovery.

Something that Devin and I have become passionate about now is following through with people not only on the beginning of their journeys but seeing it through until the end. Sticking with people when the drama is happening is easy; sitting with someone when they are struggling in the thick of recovery is extremely difficult.

Seeing someone battle the same war over and over is exhausting but sticking around is harder.

*"There are so many ways to feel utterly alone—even when you're surrounded by people.*

*Feeling misunderstood, unheard, unappreciated, unloved, unimportant.*

*Some of us might feel more lonely around people than we ever do when we're actually alone."*[1]

- Dr. Glenn Patrick Doyle

This is something that I wish I would have been warned about before going through this year, because this road can get messy and lonely very quickly. I don't think I ever realized before our crash how many people will be involved when your life is in danger and on the line, but at the same rate how many will step to the side when you get to the actual recovering part. That's where it gets uncomfortable. But I want to speak into this because especially those of us who are Christ followers, we need to sit with those and be like the example Jesus set for us. We show His love when we show up and sit side by side with someone who is grieving, when we hold the hand of someone angry with their situation. When we clean the house of someone being torn up with the battle of their mind. When we check in on those who are seemingly quiet. When we say we will be there and live it out by staying. This is the life Christ lived, and this is how we should be living our lives out too.

Have you read the story in the Bible about the man who was in need of healing and his friends were the ones who carried him to Jesus? I love this story here in Mark 2:1-5:

> *A few days later, when Jesus again entered Capernaum, the people heard that he had come home. They gathered in such large numbers that there was no room left, not even outside the door, and he preached the word to them. Some men came, bringing to him a paralyzed man, carried by four of them. Since they could not get him to Jesus because of the crowd, they made an opening in the roof above Jesus by digging through it and then lowered the mat the man was lying on. When Jesus saw their faith, he said to the paralyzed man, "Son, your sins are forgiven."*

A few notes on these verses: I love the attitudes that these friends of the paralyzed man had. They weren't going to let an annoying crowd that seemed overwhelming get in the way of the hopes they had for their friend. They didn't set the man down and say, "Aw, bummer; looks like this is actually going to be too hard, and I've actually got other plans tonight, and I wasn't expecting this to take so long. So I need to take off."

No, instead they fought through the inconvenience and stopped at nothing to get this man the healing they knew he could get from Jesus. I think this is important to note when we look at our circle. Who are the people that you surround yourself with? Are they people who bring you down and often brush off your feelings when you open up about struggling? Do they look at it as weakness when you share your vulnerability? Or are they friends that see the messy, difficult parts of your journey, those who see your brokenness and not just sit with you but want so much more for you? We need friends that have faith in our healing and can be the ones to believe and bring us to Jesus when we are too broken and can't do it ourselves.

Committed friendships don't happen overnight. I never expected every single person that reached out to us while we were in the hospital would suddenly be there for us every step of the way, holding our hands. I do, however, think it's important that we learn to understand the different types of relationships we have in our lives.

There are those who we are called to love on and be beacons of hope for in their dark times, those who we are meant to show our stories with. And while asking for prayer, our main goal should be to point them to Jesus as a way to serve them without anticipating anything in return.

I also think that on the flip side, we do need people who we can count on to stand with us in our brokenness that we can share with when we are struggling in our beliefs so that they can remind us of who we are in Christ. We need relationships with those who are willing to reach down in the mud of our messy broken parts and get a little dirty in order to pick us up so that we can find our footing again.

No matter what, it's important to remember that even when you have a close circle, they will not be with you every waking moment. They won't be able to fully understand the battle inside of your mind. And in those moments, we aren't supposed to expect them to be our helping hand 24/7. Instead, while they are there to be on the sidelines, we have the Spirit of the One who says He will never leave or abandon us. He sees and knows our hearts. He understands what we are battling, because He was once a man who battled those same things. And while we can't see Him, and it's hard to talk with someone we may not be able to see and hear back from, He is still here with each of us in this war, fighting on our behalf. Our job isn't to understand every circumstance, but to trust that He holds every situation we are walking through and is interceding on our behalf.

I've heard it said a lot from people that they just don't know how to be there for someone battling grief, depression, anxiety, or the like. That they found it was easier to just stay out of it and step to the side. Now while battling these mental health wars is exhausting, a huge side effect of this is isolating. When I've been in my deepest pits, I can't leave the house. I'm thankful if I'm able to make it out of my bed. And in these major times of battle, those are when I've lost a lot of people I love in my life.

There are those who have chosen to step away because of not knowing what to do, or not understanding that this war is something different that's beyond the control of the person facing it. And I've continued to hear story after story of people in my life who have struggled with war and have had so many people walk away from them, claiming, "Well, I didn't know how to help." This is something I find super important to talk about here in this chapter. While you may not know how to help, I can tell you with absolute certainty the one thing that will absolutely not help and, in fact, make the person's mental health battle worse, is walking away and leaving them alone.

I've struggled hardcore with isolation. I've wrestled with hurt and frustration when someone texts me, "Well, just let me know if you need anything." For those stuck in our heads, we don't know what we need. We would love a break, but that isn't really possible with this mind battle. And while it comes from good intentions, it only makes us feel worse when we can't even identify what we need. Something I've found most helpful in my journey is when people do things to help me, even if they are totally off the wall and not a priority. Because it's just something.

Devin is really good at this. If he finds me slipping into a dark swell, he'll often catch me and suggest we complete a to-do list item, or go grab some random groceries, or offer to give me a back massage. My little sister Jae is really great at checking in on me even from halfway across the country. She'll message me every week with a simple message, making sure I'm doing okay in my head and opening the door for me if I feel the need to open up and talk in a safe zone with her. My dad is really great about making sure that I'm not only taking care of my mind but helping my mind in this battle by getting me out to exercise. He knew that I wanted to start running again, and as soon as I was cleared this past summer by my spinal doctor, my dad began picking me up and going running with me weekly at the beach. He didn't just encourage me to get back into running; he came alongside me in it.

My friend Katie has been a great support in this as well. She was someone who came into the ICU at the hospital with a basket full of snacks and murder mystery books (which she got me hooked on). She followed through during our recovery, and when I went to rehab, she heard I needed new clothes in order to fit around my new gear for my injuries and went out and practically bought me a whole new wardrobe, delivering it to Devin to bring to me. She has continued to follow through weekly with me, by taking me out on runs and hikes, and not only being there to encourage me in getting back into physical strengths but has been an open ear as I sort through the messiness inside my head. She also offers an understanding heart along the way.

My older sister Bry has come alongside us, also from halfway across the country, and motivated us in our journey, whether it's by sending funny memes or jokes to us or checking in to make sure we're feeling okay during days when she knows we are struggling physically. She often encourages us to do Bible studies together and motivates me to get deep into studies to learn more about Christ. And perhaps one of the simplest yet most meaningful things she did was on our year anniversary of our accident last week; she knew it was an emotional day, and we were struggling with the shock and all that has come our way this year. She simply sent a donation to us, telling us to go get some dessert to celebrate our survival day. This was something just extremely thoughtful and made us feel loved in knowing that there is someone out there who is happy we are still alive.

These are just a few of the people in our circle who are praying for us and taking on the battle alongside us as we walk through it. Even if they aren't all here physically beside us.

Because it is easy to be there when you can see the physical injuries. When there's blood, stitches, and tubes, it's easy to send flowers when someone is lying in a hospital bed. It's easy to say, "Take your time" and not expect anything from someone when they are medicated, and a wheelchair sits beside their bed. It's easy to say you are someone's friend when their accident is on the headline news. It's easy to share a news video link or GoFundMe when you want to be a part of the in crowd as the drama plays out.

It's hard to be there for someone whose life got flipped upside down. It's hard to sit with someone while they are grieving. It's hard to be there for someone suffering from their own mind attacking them at all hours of the day. It's hard to understand when someone is suffering from not only broken bones but a broken brain. It's hard to love someone who can't always get out of bed, who can no longer initiate plans, or is physically exhausted from their body and mind tormenting them. These things are hard ... but that doesn't mean they aren't doable.

We have to be willing to see the deepest and yuckiest parts of people in order to truly love them for who they are, and we have the ultimate example because this is exactly what Christ has done for us. I was having a conversation with Devin about this shortly into our recovery, and I actually wrote a post about it online that I think relates to all we've been talking about here. I titled this post "Insides." Here's what I wrote:

*Insides*

*I was telling Devin a while back that it's really weird to think about our surgeons seeing our insides.*

*When I go in for a follow-up and shake the hand of someone that was once holding my guts in and seeing my inmost dirtiest parts, I can't help but feel a little odd of embarrassed.*

*But the surgeons never run away. (I mean they do want their paycheck.)*

*They see the messy broken stuff and mend it together so we can be repaired and new.*

*I was thinking this is a cool, little example of how God is with us too...*

*He sees our yuckiest insides of our hearts that are filled with so much sin and stuff that would gross anyone else out.*

*He doesn't run.*

*He changes things around, moves the guts and blood around (not literally lol) to make it so that we feel anew ... and from there, after surgery, we can't just continue now with life as before...*

*We are fixed because we are changed and have a new way of living so we don't continue damaging our bodies...*

*And just like instructions are given for a new way of using our bodies after surgery, God gives us instructions on the new way to live when we accept Him into our lives. His instructions are there to protect us from further harm and to help repair our brokenness and previous injuries.*

*Surgeons don't tell us not to do something to ruin our lives—they do it to keep us safe. So how much more does God love and care for us since He gives us His Word with instructions to live and protect us! So cool!*

*"Therefore, if anyone is in Christ, the new creation has come: the old has gone, the new is here!" 2 Corinthians 5:17*

*"Search me, God, and know my heart; test me and know my anxious thoughts. See if there is any offensive way in me, and lead me in the way everlasting." Psalm 139:23-24*

*"The LORD does not look at the things people look at. People look at the outward appearance, but the LORD looks at the heart." 1 Samuel 16:7*

So, I encourage you today ... be like Jesus and stick around through the messes that those you love are facing. Challenge them to remember what Christ has done before and can do again, and share hope when they are struggling in their faith. From someone who has both walked in the valleys of grief, recovery, and trauma, and who has also walked through many valleys with people I love facing similar wars, it gets really dark, and the weariness seems unending at times. I have gotten frustrated in situations with myself, and I know I'm not the only one who feels like our minds are on a loop of constantly reliving the trauma that we've been through. I get mad at myself if I'm bringing it up again in conversation with someone who has already heard it before. But I think it's important to know that when your loved one is bringing up things like this and the battle they are struggling with, it's not to continue to live in the past.

I think it's an important way that we are trying to bring you in and share our darkest parts of what we are battling. And somehow bringing it to light and out of the darkness of the secret places of our minds makes it just a little easier to take on.

*"No complex trauma survivor is trying to 'live in the past.' LOTS of complex trauma survivors feel TRAPPED in the past—and would give*

*ANYTHING to never 'go' there again. If they talk about it because they're trying to find their way OUT of the maze."*² *- Dr. Glenn Patrick Doyle*

I'll begin wrapping this chapter up, but I want to drive home the point that while we are going to struggle here on earth and will never understand true, unconditional love apart from Christ, we will be hurt by people, and others will reject us. We will lose friends, family might ignore us, coworkers talk bad about us. We have every right to feel and grieve those hurts and losses. But something that we must remember is that while we are rejected by those on earth, we are handpicked and chosen by the One who created our inmost parts. One of my favorite verses is in John 15:16. It reads:

"*You did not choose me, but I chose you and appointed you so that you might go and bear fruit—fruit that will last—and so that whatever you ask in my name the Father will give you.*"

Whenever I'm struggling with feeling lost in the world and that others aren't wanting me, I take comfort in knowing that even when the God who made you and me, and everything in the universe; while He doesn't need us, He still wants us—and chooses us to be in a relationship with Him. He doesn't need us in order to accomplish anything or to be fulfilled. But because He loves us so much as His kids, He chooses us so that we can experience true love and what it means to be pursued by someone wholeheartedly. He died for us so that we wouldn't have to live without Him.

I have this tattoo on my left wrist. Well, I wanted it on my left ring finger, or wedding ring finger originally, but the tattoo artist insisted it would be too painful for me and suggested the wrist instead. I got this when I was nineteen, and before I was engaged or married yet. My idea with this tattoo was wanting it before I got married and to hold it as a testimony I could share with others that I was chosen by God. My tattoo reads "Bride of Christ." It's rooted in the story of the Last Supper in the Bible and takes place as Jesus shares this last meal with His disciples.

Throughout my life, I have been turned down, rejected, and have been chosen second by people of this world rather than being their first choice. But in my teenage years, God started showing me that He called me His own, that I was His and chosen. This relates to the idea in Luke 22 when Jesus is sharing the Last Supper with the disciples. Jesus offers them the cup, which He says, "is the new covenant poured out for you." Now, what a lot of people miss here is that when Jesus is offering His disciples this cup, it isn't just some ordinary wine glass. This is the cup of salvation.

So, when He presents this to them, and is offering it to them, He is asking them to be His bride. This cup is the same cup that Jews would use when a man was going to ask a woman to be his wife! When a Jewish man was going to propose to a woman, they would gather in the home with their families on both sides. The families would sit with this man and woman around the table. And the man would then offer this cup to the woman, and if she took it and drank of it, that would mean she was accepting his proposal.

Now after this proposal would take place, the groom would then need to go away and back to his hometown for a while. He would go to build onto his family's house an expansion, or better known as a "mansion." When he went away to build this mansion, the bride would be waiting back at home and would not know the day or the hour when the groom would be coming back for her to marry her.

But when the groom would come back, this would be a celebration! There would be trumpets, horns, and a huge ceremony! Now, does this sound like something you may have heard about in Scripture? Where Christ talks about how He will return for us some day, even when we do not know when or where?

Jesus offers His disciples, and us, this cup of salvation. We have the opportunity to be His bride and accept His proposal. And when we accept it, we learn that He came and died for us, and He is going away for a while. But while He is gone, He is busy building onto His Father's house our mansions, where we will live with Him someday. And just as the bride in Jewish culture doesn't know the return date of the groom, we also don't know when our groom will return. But we know that it will be a celebration because He is coming back for us someday—His chosen people, His loves, His Bride.

The beautiful thing in all of this is that He isn't forcing us to take this cup. He offers it to us freely, knowing full well in His heart that we may reject it. He loves us so much though that He will still have His heart broken by being rejected by us, rather than not offering it to us at all.

So, I want to give you this hope—we will constantly be turned down here, but we can accept the gift of salvation of the One who wants us and loves us so deeply. This doesn't make our lives perfect here, and there will be days of loneliness while waiting for His return. But we can have full hope and faith that He will not forget us nor abandon us. He loves us unconditionally and will always pursue and choose us.

"In the same way, after the supper he took the cup, saying, 'This cup is the new covenant in my blood, which is poured out for you.'" Luke 22:20

"For you are a people holy to the LORD your God, and the LORD has chosen you to be a people for his treasured possession, out of all the peoples who are on the face of the earth." Deuteronomy 14:2

"You were chosen by God the Father long ago. He knew you were to become His children. You were set apart for holy living by the Holy Spirit. May you obey Jesus Christ and be made clean by His blood. May you be full of His love-favor and peace." 1 Peter 1:2

"But you are a chosen people, a royal priesthood, a holy nation, God's special possession, that you may declare the praises of him who called you out of darkness into his wonderful light."

1 Peter 2:9

"Therefore, as God's chosen people, holy and dearly loved, clothe yourselves with compassion, kindness, humility, gentleness, and patience." Colossians 3:12

"God chose the lowly things of this world and the despised things—and the things that are not—to nullify the things that are, so that no one may boast before him." 1 Corinthians 1:28-29

"All the praise to God, the Father of our Lord Jesus Christ, who has blessed us with every spiritual blessing in the heavenly realms because we are united with Christ. Even before he made the world, God loved us and chose us in Christ to be holy and without fault in his eyes." Ephesians 1:3-4

"If you belonged to the world, it would love you as its own. As it is, you do not belong to the world, but I have chosen you out of the world. That is why the world hates you." John 15:19

"All those the Father gives me will come to me, and whoever comes to me I will never drive away. For I have come down from heaven not to do my will but to do the will of him who sent me. And this is the will of him who sent me, that I shall lose none of all those he has give me, but raise them up *at the last day. For my Father's will is that everyone who looks to the Son and believes in him shall have eternal life, and I will raise them up at the last day." John 6:37-40*

# Chapter 10: Some Tough Questions

*"Within the valleys of our grief, something beautiful wants to grow. Tend those fields, water those little seeds. What was planted in pain, can harvest beautiful possibilities."*
[1] - Mike Foster

THOSE TOUGH QUESTIONS, MAN ... they are something else. Something I didn't realize was the number of questions and comments that come your way after experiencing something so traumatic. I never thought about having to learn to filter the rude questions and/or comments that people will say simply to just do that, to just say it. I've felt like I have needed to grow an extra layer of skin to get through this last year with some of the things that have been said in our direction. A lot of the time I don't know how to respond, especially if grief or tough emotions have been triggered and leave me stuck. But God has been teaching me to grow in this area in some new ways.

### *"Well, it's a good thing you don't have kids that were in the car with you!"*

No, we didn't have kids with us in the car. It's been odd to me how often this has been said to us during our recovery. Oftentimes after someone hears our story, this is their conclusion to why we need to be thankful. The first few times I think it really rubbed me the wrong way. In a way, it made me feel small, like it was a blow thrown at us for not being as important as this imaginary child someone had in their head. I felt like we were basically being told, "Well, you aren't as important as a kid, so you should be thankful there wasn't a child with you."

Honestly, I still don't really have a great response for this. I usually just awkwardly smile through it. But it's also triggered some tough grief when we've been told this. Because while others may not understand the way we feel, Enya was our baby; we did lose our kid in our crash. And I think the more I've stepped back from the question, I realized how offended and misunderstood I was feeling when someone doesn't put those two pieces of information together.

But when I look at the whole picture, I'm learning that yes, people will say silly things just to say it. It's often not helpful, but nine times out of ten, it isn't a targeted attack on me, even when the enemy is telling me to take offense and to live in bitterness and anger. Some people just say comments to gain more information, whether out of selfish reasons to fill their own minds or something else. But even if it is selfish, I'm trying to learn to have grace and not take it as a personal attack. The enemy would love for division and bitterness to be stirred up and held onto. We can't give him that foothold to grip onto. We must forgive quickly and listen quicker.

*"Know this, my beloved brothers: let every person be quick to hear, slow to speak, slow to anger; for the anger of man does not produce the righteousness of God." James 1:19-20*

*"Whoever is slow to anger has great understanding, but he who has a hasty temper exalts folly." Proverbs 14:29*

"Good sense makes one slow to anger, and it is his glory to overlook an offense." Proverbs 19:11

"Be not quick in your spirit to become angry, for anger lodges in the bosom of fools." Ecclesiastes 7:9

"A hot-tempered man stirs up strife, but he who is slow to anger quiets contention." Proverbs 15:18

"Be angry and do not sin; do not let the sun go down on your anger, and give no opportunity to the devil." Ephesians 4:26-27

We can be angry and upset, but it's what we do with those emotions and where we store them that we must be cautious of. It's okay to feel hurt, but the way we respond matters. Is our response love, or is it a harsh tone? Is it forgiveness, or the decision to cut off and dismiss the relationship? Being hurt is okay, but in our anger that God allows us to have, we must seek love in spite of it. He is quick to overlook our mistakes and faults in life. So being a follower of Him means following Him with that same response.

### *"When are you going to get a new dog?"*

This one gets me every single time; this is where I freeze. It's hard to fake your way through a conversation that hurts. It's difficult to hold back tears when emotions want to flood out. It's painful to talk about something that feels personal, that holds vulnerability and pain all at once. I think that in a lot of ways, some people try to ask me this because they know how much we have been grieving losing Enya. It's some people's way of trying to bring a fix they think will cure the situation we are facing. But that isn't the fix, and it won't heal the pain of losing someone we loved so dearly. I heard it said this way recently:

*"Grief is like surfing. Except you're blindfolded. In a hurricane. And your surfboard is on fire. And the people on the shore are shouting surfing strategies for a storm they've never surfed and then shaking their heads at how you handle the waves."*[2] *- (Anonymous)*

If I spoke my mind on this question, I'd probably tell people to be more sensitive, and in all honesty, it's not really their business if or when we ever get another dog. The question in itself doesn't make a whole lot of sense to me. When someone loses someone, a family member or friend to a disease, my conclusion to try to help the person never requires me asking when they will get a new family member or when will they get a new friend. So why is that the go-to solution here? I don't have the answer to this yet. And it's still a difficult conversation for me to navigate through, almost always leaving me walking through it in tears. It requires a lot of God's grace and Him whispering to me to hold back anger and frustration, to hold things that aren't of Him back.

Recently though, I had an encounter on this topic that really softened my heart, and I believe God used it to help me form a new thought pattern and how to respond to this question better. My little nephew Bear came up to me about a month ago. He was just days away from his sixth birthday, and I swear he just gets cuter every single day! Bear is the perfect example of what it means to care for someone. My sister talks about how much he was there for her when she had her most recent baby. At the midwife center, she describes how Bear held her hand and comforted her throughout her labor; what a sweet support system he was, and how much he cared to be there for his mom when she was in so much pain.

So now that you have a glimpse into little Bear's personality, you can see how my mind went through a loop when Bear looks up at me with his big blue eyes, while holding both my hands, and asks me, "Auntie Jo, are you going to get a new doggie?" I've been asked this so many times in the last year. Most don't realize the triggering thoughts it causes Devin and me to have. I feel confused as to why Enya seems like something that can be replaced. When encountered with this question, I usually try to rush out of the conversation. I don't want someone trying to fix something that isn't theirs. My heart has a hard time absorbing all of this at once.

But when my sweet nephew asked me this, I froze in place. I was in a predicament. I had no desire to flee the conversation; I welcome all conversations with my nieces and nephews. I'm always eager to learn about and with them. I want to hear how their little minds are brainstorming, why they tick the way they do, and learn more deeply about them so I can love them in the ways they need.

So there I stood, in the middle of a Midwest Fleet Farm, holding tiny little hands and looking into the curious eyes of a little boy who loves his Auntie Jo so much. Who I know has no intent to hurt me. Who I know loved Enya and also grieves the loss of her. I have this little human that I love so dang much, and I lost the ability to speak. I was at a loss for words.

After catching my bearings and wiping away some tears from my watering eyes, I got down on my knees to Bear's eye level and looked him in the eyes to respond to his question. I told him "Not right now ... I just really miss Enya, and it hurts a lot." In my mind, this lets him know my heart is and will always hurt for her, and right now, I don't have the capacity to pour into another pup when I'm in the midst of so much grief and healing. That I wouldn't be the best I could be for another dog.

Bear responded back as soon as he saw the tears in my eyes, "Well, you could get another Eny-dog (what he calls a Golden Retriever) and name it Enya too!" My heart shattered … I wrapped this sweet, little boy tightly in my embrace.

When an adult has brushed aside my feelings and my grief, I've been told to just get another "special dog." And in those conversations, I have no desire to continue talking. But there is something that stirs up your heart when the naiveness of a child asks the tough questions. Those are the moments that I believe allow you to work through tough things in the best of ways. Anger gets set aside because children aren't trying to hurt you. Bear's intent was never to make his aunt hurt.

Grief is a really tricky thing … people often don't know what to say and I often don't know how to respond. But through this conversation with Bear, I was reminded of this verse in the Bible:

"…*Truly I tell you, unless you change and become like little children, you will never enter the kingdom of heaven.*" Matthew 18:3

Jesus gives us some cool tools here that can help to walk with others through grief. We should approach those hurting with the intentions and the vulnerability of a child. Bear offered a suggestion—in his heart, this would help his Auntie Jo's heart. And while people may ask the same question while being adults, the intentions don't seem to me to be with the same attitude and caring heart that Bear had.

I walked away from that conversation with him learning how to be more careful with my words when I approach someone who is grieving. And I think I've learned that we should all be a lot more like Bear, more like Jesus, and seek to walk with others through their paths of grief instead of trying to fix everything that isn't even our duty to fix. Our focus should be to care, not to cure.

### "Have you tried melatonin?"

Alright, this one may seem a little silly. Honestly, I've gotten this question for years, even before our car accident. Once people catch the fact that I don't sleep at night, melatonin is their quick response in an attempt to heal all my lifelong sleep issues. It honestly doesn't really upset me; it just makes me tired with the idea of having to go through the conversation again about my attempts at taking it, and that it's a far greater issue than the melatonin levels in my body. I think again that this is a way that others think they can cure a problem, and a suggestion they feel is appropriate to offer.

It's currently around six a.m. I actually slept for a couple of hours last night. That's pretty huge for me. My sleep pattern usually consists of being up all night and napping for a few hours at some point during the day, if I have the time and availability. I don't like this schedule, because it makes me feel like I'm missing out on a lot in life. It used to be something I could push through. But now with my physical injuries limiting my body and causing new pains, I don't know how to push on through a body I don't recognize anymore.

I know a lot of people who take melatonin for sleep, and it works amazing for them. And I think there's a part of me that feels like a failure when something that works so well for some has absolutely no effect on me. When the hardcore sleep medications my psychologist had prescribed had no effect, or even worse, bad side effects on top of not helping me sleep, I began feeling extremely down on myself and embarrassed by how terrible my body and mind are thrown off that they don't allow me to have true rest at night.

I think something that I've had to learn along the way and be reminded of in Christ is that my value and worth aren't placed in what I produce or how productive I am each day. Often when I have really bad episodes where I'm not sleeping at all, when I'm days into absolutely no sleep, and no matter what I try I cannot pass out, I feel crazy. At that point, anxiety becomes strong. Physically, my body reacts by a rapid heartbeat, and feelings of paranoia kick in at all-time highs. This is a common cycle for me. It's weekly. And finally at some point, I crash into a deep nap, and that usually resets my body until the next cycle of sleeplessness for the rest of the week. This is how my body works; this is my normal.

I think it frustrates a lot of people to learn this about me. They often want to come in and try to take a crack at diagnosing me, or asking me why the normal bedtime routines, remedies, or even medications don't work. And my answer is always "I don't know." This is a lifelong struggle, not just something that happened from our crash. But admittedly, it has become far worse since our accident. There are now more things to worry about, more for my mind to replay all night, more grief to battle.

It makes me sad honestly. The fact that I feel like I let people down when we go through the list of how much my body seems to fail at this rest. How much I have seemed to have failed at this rest. But I'm learning to keep in mind that it's just a way people are trying to offer help. I don't think it comes from a place of ill intent. But I write this to try to encourage others to be careful and mindful of the words and questions that you bring to those struggling with chronic illnesses. There's a lot we don't have answers to and maybe never will in our lifetimes. And although that's frustrating a lot of the time, this is the road we are on, and I have to believe that there is something God is teaching me and will hopefully use for His glory one day.

I think it is important to keep in mind how we respond to those struggling with these difficult things and not come in with the intention of trying to have all the answers. Simply offering condolences on the issue may be all there is to offer, and that is okay! In the same way, we don't go up to someone who is battling cancer, an infectious disease, or physical limitations and ask them why they aren't cured yet, why the medication isn't working, why the chemotherapy isn't taking effect, why they don't try x, y, or z, etc. It's crucial to keep this in mind with chronic illness, mental illnesses, and the like: they are real diseases too. And in the same way not all infections get cured or respond to medication correctly, so is the same with these areas of sickness as well.

I think I find it most difficult to accept that this may be a lifelong struggle for me. It's hard battling exhaustion. It's hard to recover physically and mentally when your mind desperately needs rest. I'm often misunderstood. I've often been looked down upon when I've had to take seasons off from not working full time, or even at all. I think people don't like the idea that Devin needs to support us both, like I'm lazy or not holding up my end of the stick in our marriage. This shouldn't bother me, but it still does. It always has. I've been told that I need to step up, that I'm not doing enough, and that I shouldn't be making Devin do all this.

When in reality, Devin never has felt that way. Often, he's the one encouraging me to seek any kind of rest I can. To not push myself, that I don't need to work, and that he will provide for us. And that is what I should be hearing and listening to. But the harsh comments and the looks I receive when I'm out of work paralyzes me with the label of "failure" and makes me hate the way that I am.

It was interesting when we went through the car accident though. There were a few months where everyone was understanding. I wasn't expected for the first time in my life to be productive or work. I was told by every person around me to seek rest in order to recover. And I look back at it all now, and that mindset in the eyes of others quickly changed when they saw that my body was beginning to heal. But my question is why do people need to see you physically struggling in order to tell you to rest? Why isn't mental health as important as our physical health in our culture today? Why is someone who is struggling and battling getting out of bed each day labeled as lazy or unmotivated?

And that's the thing. I'm far from being unmotivated. I do everything in my power to be productive and help our family out, even if some days that's from under the covers in bed. And I'm definitely not lazy. If I'm not moving, if I'm not on top of things and feeling like things are continuing to move in life, it drives me up the wall. It always has. But I also struggle for my mind and body to keep up with the productivity my thoughts and desires want in life. I look down on myself more than anything and push myself far beyond limits in order to try to keep up with the world's standards. I want to work full time; heck, that would be life-changing for us if I could bring in a reliable second income. But that's not reality. And I'm learning that even when I may not have understanding from peers, or the society around me, maybe God is still calling me to enter into His rest with Him. Will I be misunderstood? Absolutely. Will it matter in eternity though? Not at all.

This is something I continue to struggle with, but instead of letting it take over and live in the idea that I'm a failure as an adult, God has been teaching me over this last year to learn how to rest in ways, even if it doesn't necessarily mean sleeping. It meant learning to say no when all I did before was say yes. It means still battling the views of others but fighting past those thoughts that could easily tear me down and, inside, realizing that rest is a holy thing and what God is calling me to right now.

*"Come to me, all you who are weary and burdened, and I will give you rest. Take my yoke upon you and learn from me; for I am gentle and humble in heart, and you will find rest for your souls. For my yoke is easy and my burden is light."* Matthew 11:28-30

Rest may not mean getting into a REM cycle. It might mean coming to Christ in our feelings of failure and unworthiness and simply laying down. It might look like taking time off work in order to prioritize a walk each day. Maybe that is all you can physically handle. And that step is huge and enough! It's important to lean into the rest that Christ is allowing you to have, not fighting it. I'm still learning that I need certain areas of rest, and I still struggle with not feeling guilty over it. Some days I will not keep up with everyone around me. Some days I will struggle and not be able to move. And other days I can blow through my entire to-do list, take a run, and still accomplish more. But in the middle of it all, rest is needed to keep going and, ultimately, to make it possible to say yes to the things that God has in store for us.

Throughout our recovery over this past year, Christ has been teaching me a lot on this topic of rest. I still have so much to learn, and often still battle the idea that this is a holy thing to be able to sit at His feet, even if that means taking a nap. Because that nap might be needed in order to help something or someone He has in mind for me to help later on that day. Rest is something He gives us in order to have energy to continue to share about His kingdom. During recovery, I entered into an online writing contest, and the topic was on "REST." I didn't win the contest, but I think writing about the idea of it all really helped me process the things God was beginning to teach me through it all. I want to share it with you here. I wrote:

#Rest

*"When he has brought me to what I felt was a 'holding' place while everyone around me continued to move on. Their lives kept going, and I was going to have a lot of catching up to do...*

*Wouldn't you rather be waiting in a season the LORD has prepared for you, rather than moving on in a season He did not create for you?"*[3] *- Krystal Ribble*

*I used to think rest meant sleeping in and being lazy, ignoring to-do lists and being unavailable to others.*

*I ran in the opposite direction of these things every day. I fought hard to not be okay with the idea of rest. In my mind, it meant not serving the kingdom of God.*

*It seemed selfish and failing to love others in the ways they needed.*

*I convinced myself that serving Christ meant never taking a break until I'm in heaven. And even then, it would be a new kind of service to the Lord when I'm getting to see Him every day.*

*I worked at multiple jobs for as long as I can remember. Obsessing over the idea that I couldn't look like a failing adult to others.*

*If I sat still, it meant I didn't measure up. It meant I wasn't keeping up with peers my age and not as much of an adult without being set in one firm career.*

*I couldn't be a failure, especially to those who have told me I was one no matter how much I juggled in life.*

*Then the crash happened...*

*The first couple weeks in the hospital, we didn't know if I'd walk again.*

*Then when I could walk again, it was go time; my mind told me I needed to get back to it.*

*It came as a shock to me that you can't do a whole lot after major spinal surgery ... my jobs were off the table. Chores and errands became physically impossible.*

*And I found myself sitting not only in physical pain but drenched in painful guilt that I couldn't do anything.*

*Recovering became my new job; it's my current occupation.*

*And not only did God allow this weird and floopy time in my life ... but He invites me to rest in it.*

*"Come to me, all you who are weary and burdened, and I will give you rest. Take my yoke upon you and learn from me, for I am gentle and humble in heart, and you will find rest for your souls. For my yoke is easy and my burden is light." Matthew 11:28-30*

*There isn't a quota or limit we have to reach in weariness to rest in Him. The life He gave us isn't intended to be spent burnt out...*

*It's meant to be lived for Him: working hard to love others, but then coming back to rest in Him so we can be filled back up and sent back out to keep serving.*

*I wrestle with God on how important it is that He heal me right now, because I want to get busy serving Him again! I plead that I feel like I'm living my life half asleep, and that's not benefiting the souls that need Jesus.*

*But then He kneels down to meet me where I am. He explains that I am enough right where I am, and I'm not as important as I think I am (in a good way).*

*His work and His will are going to happen, and my tiny part in this tournament of life has me sitting on the bench, taking a breather right now.*

*I'm not the whole team (thank God!).*

*There are other parts of this body of Christ spreading His love and sharing the message of Him.*

*So right now, I will listen to the coach (aka God)...*

*I'll take my seat on the bench. I'll accept the water He gives me to replenish and listen to the future plays He has for me when I go back in.*

*I want to be part of the action. I wanna score the game-winning run and bring others joy.*

*But for now, the best thing I can do for this team is Rest."*

*****

So, I'll wrap up this chapter with one final note. I don't have all the right answers to these questions that others are asking. Heck, I don't even have answers to most of the things I ask myself. But I'm learning and being convicted constantly that this world is not my home. I'm not meant to fit in here, and I'm not supposed to feel comfortable here. My life isn't to impress others; it's to be an example of Christ and point others to Him through my words and actions.

"Am I now trying to win the approval of human beings or of God?" Galatians 1:10

It's just not worth it to spend our days concerned or worried over the thoughts and opinions others have of our lives. I don't say that lightly, because I definitely still struggle with getting worried about what they think. But I'm trying to make the conscious effort to change that. It's costing me too much to be concerned with such things. If God is calling me to it, and this is the place He is inviting me into, then what others think doesn't matter in the end. And if I'm going to be so caught up with concerning myself about others when I'm supposed to be resting, I'm now neither being productive or getting to experience the rest God is handing over to me. This world isn't our home. We must prepare our hearts and minds with eternal mindsets, and rest is necessary to get there.

*"My home is in heaven. I'm just traveling through this world."*[4] - Billy Graham

# Chapter 11: Fear of Flying

*"What you fear reveals where you trust God the least."*[1] - Craig Groeshel

I'M AFRAID OF FLYING. Nope ... let me rephrase that ... I am deathly, can't stand, terrified, shaking in my boots, paranoid, and want to cry afraid of flying. I've always hated it, but the weird thing about it is that Devin and I travel often. We are on a plane multiple times a month. Sometimes it's for exploring new places, new states, new countries. Other times it's to go squeeze our loved ones in different states. And I used to think that I'd get more comfortable and begin to like it the more we flew. But it's actually gone in the total opposite direction.

Last week, Devin and I embarked on a new milestone ... we visited our fiftieth state!!! Throughout our time together, we have had a giant map of the United States of America that is glued to a giant canvas and has hung on our wall in whatever home, apartment, or room we are living in. As the years have gone on, when we travel to a different state, we snap a photo in front of the state sign of that state. And then when we return home, we print it out and put it in the proper state it is on our map.

It's been such a special thing we have looked forward to doing in each new state, and a great way to hold memories and cherish adventures. After many road trips, lots of plane rides, camping, backpacking, hiking, visiting loved ones, and everything in between, we visited our forty-ninth state in August of 2022. Our goal was to make it to our fiftieth state before the end of the year to complete our map and create our own club of the fifty states! So, we packed our bags, we got our tortoise a sitter for the week, booked a couple of flights, and we were on our way.

Something kind of funny about Devin and myself is that we don't ever have a real plan when it comes to our traveling. Now you might think that is just a personality quirk, but if you know me, you'll know I'm a planner. I have my calendar on me often and am constantly planning things out months in advance. I don't want to accidentally make plans with two different people on the same day and have to cancel on someone. I don't want us to be overwhelmed with twenty things to do in one day, so often I'll try to wean that down to at least nineteen (you may think I'm kidding, but I'm not haha). I want to fit everything in, so I organize, post-it note, highlight, color-code, whatever it may be to keep our lives together ... well, at least attempt to in the form of on paper.

But back to our lack of plans. We have this app we often use when we go places where if you book a hotel or motel room just minutes or a couple hours before you arrive there, you actually end up saving a pretty hefty amount of money. We've gotten rooms for more than half off their original price. We sometimes do something similar with flights. It's definitely more of a gamble, but we've found that if we book our flights the week of (or, in some cases, we are guilty of booking a flight the day of), we've also been able to save a bit.

This drives people bananas; I know this because everyone tells us. When we announce we're going on a trip, the question that follows is usually, "Where are you staying?" which we reply, "I don't know yet." Or the next question, "When are you coming home?" Devin and I usually look at each other and respond with something along the lines of "We'll see, we'll let ya know!" And while I know this freaks people out, it's also something that I really love about us. Because we are this way, on nearly every one of our trips, we end up somewhere we didn't expect, and those are some of my favorite memories to bring home over the years.

So, circling back to our trip this past week. We got on our first flight with the destination of Seattle. I was miserable and anxious the whole flight. I'm very hyper aware of every sound the engine makes, or when it stops making noise and I begin to think the plane is going down. I'm constantly on the lookout for flight attendants to see their reactions to noises or bumps along the way caused by turbulence. Before we get on flights, I'm always staring down at the pilot if I can catch a glimpse of him before take-off. My concerns are always, "Did he sleep last night or is he going to fall asleep flying this thing? Is he upset about anything right now or angry where he won't be able to think properly and operate this flight? Does he look tired? Can someone please get this man a coffee so this plane stays in the air?!"

In case you're wondering, no, I'm not being dramatic or over exaggerating. I go through all of this every single flight. When we arrived in Seattle, Washington, we spent the day in one of our favorite little cities. We spent one of our anniversaries in Seattle years back, and since then, it's been a very special place we look forward to visiting. We love Pike Market Place, from the fish being thrown from fisherman to fisherman, to the coffee, smell of fresh flowers, and the funny people you see along the way: it's an atmosphere we highly recommend visiting if you haven't yet.

After walking through the city streets, grabbing food in the marketplace, browsing every bookstore shelf I could get my hands on, and making the climb up some hefty hills in the streets, we began our train ride back to our hotel for the evening. As the evening went on, I was growing increasingly anxious. I was so excited that we would be arriving in Alaska the next day, but I was also dreading the plane rides that were coming. Our flight itinerary had us on a tiny plane for our first flight, which would fly from Seattle to Portland, Oregon. This kind of ticked me off that we were going backward and had to add the extra flight just to catch a ride to Alaska, but I tried to stick to my thoughts on the long-term goal.

But with each flight, I became more anxious; I cried more tears; I was absolutely convinced that we were on a plane where the engine was breaking, or we were going to hit a flock of birds, or the pilot didn't know what he was doing. It sounds bizarre when I'm writing this, but I know that the next plane ride I get on, I'm going to be convinced all over again. And that's the crazy thing about fear and anxiety. It speaks lies through things that seem like they are so incredibly close to the truth.

I often reason on an airplane with myself, *Okay, so everyone says that planes are safer than cars. But wait, I've been in a car accident, so this must put me at a higher risk for crashing in this plane! Okay, now, Jo ... we aren't good at statistics. Maybe this isn't how this all works.* Then I take a few breaths in while holding my ears tightly, trying to block out all the sounds of the plane, the wind, and everything else around. I try to calm my body down because now I'm nauseous, most likely because we're moving in weird motions on the plane and I'm forgetting to breathe.

So, then I go on trying to reason with myself again: *Okay, Devin says everything is okay and that everything is normal. He told me to look at the flight attendants, so I looked at them and they don't seem concerned. Actually, they are just laughing about something. But wait, maybe if something is wrong with the plane, they don't hear it because they are too distracted by whatever it is that they are talking about and laughing. Maybe I should tell someone that the plane doesn't sound right. No, that sounds crazy.*

At some point on the flights, I end up trying to breathe again. Usually at this point we've been off the ground for a measly six minutes. I'm feeling the pressure of being pointed up toward the sky, my body is being pushed back in my seat; my feet are feeling weird, like they could be raised up at any second, so I'm trying to keep them planted on the ground. The engines are getting really loud (which, as I'm sitting on my couch, makes sense to me because an engine is going to be working harder now that it's off the ground and actually flying). This is freaking me out because why wasn't it this loud when we were in line to take off on the runway? My heart beats ... nope, beats isn't a strong enough word. My heart thuds, and I feel it in my chest, my throat, and my stomach. I try to tell it to calm down; it doesn't. The rest of my body responds to this thudding, and everything starts shaking. I can't control my hands, while my right leg is always the one that starts shaking dramatically.

And now I find myself ten minutes into a flight in a full-blown panic attack. My body won't listen to my mind trying to calm it down. Before my anxiety takes over, I have a few minutes of reassuring it that everything will be okay. But I'm usually on a time crunch. My mind has to speak its soothing and reassurance quickly before my body takes over. But time and time again, my body keeps winning. I tell myself, *It's okay; God is in control of this flight,* hoping that this releases some of the tension. But then I remember, *Wait, God never promised me that this flight wasn't going to crash. In the same way He didn't promise to protect me from a car accident. So, if He didn't promise me, then this plane could very well go down at any moment here.*

This is the pattern of thoughts, of feelings, of emotions, and of physical things I face every single take-off. I think my body thinks it's funny to go into "fight or flight" on every flight as a way to make a pun. But in all seriousness, this has become a really big hurdle in my life. I know that a big part of the fear stems from PTSD, and I know it's gotten worse since our car accident. I know that I don't like being in any kind of motor vehicle now, and that the slightest noise or movement that sounds off can send me into a breakdown and flashbacks of our accident at any given moment.

My therapist once said to me: "We can't change history, but we can change how our brain stores it."

And that is something I'm really trying to work on. Because while I can't change what happened with our car accident and, at the same time, no, I cannot control the airplane I'm going to fly on in a few weeks, or the car someone is driving me in, my body has a way that it responded in our crash. Now it overcompensates and wants to try to control any threats of fear in order to keep me from danger or something bad happening to me again.

It's hard for me to talk about my fear of flying. Not only because it's embarrassing, but the big thing that gets me is that I feel like people look at me as someone who doesn't trust God because of it.

And honestly, that doesn't have anything to do with it. I know God loves me and doesn't wish any harm on me. But at the same time, I know that He allows hard things to happen, and He doesn't make any promises to extend my life until the next day. He promises to protect me, but that isn't about my physical life here on earth. He is protecting my heart and soul, and no matter what happens to me here on earth, I know for certain that my eternity will be spent with Him in heaven at the end of it all.

And while I know this confidently, I'm still terrified of airplanes. I don't like the rocking, the loud noises, the vibrating in the seats when the engine is revving up. I don't like knowing that even if the plane did go down, and I died, I don't like the fact that I'd still have to experience the falling from thousands of feet into the air, eventually crashing, and having to go through all of that before meeting Christ. Maybe that sounds silly, but it's the way my mind works.

My sister Bry sent me a meme this morning that I find is appropriate to add into this section. The meme says:

"Having anxiety is like being in an argument with an idiot and the idiot is winning. No matter how stupid what they say is, it's really persuasive.

Anxiety: "Hey what if..."

Me: "Lol that could never happen"

Anxiety: "Haha yeah. But what if it did?"

Me: "Oh my gosh you're right!"[2]

I feel like this is such an excellent representation of living with anxiety, constantly living in a world of "what ifs." And while I'm working through this journey of not allowing it to control my life, as I know many of you out there are as well, I do think there are differences in what is stored in our minds and what is stored in our bodies when facing anxiety. Let me elaborate a bit on that. What I mean to say is that like I mentioned before, often before my body starts going into a panic, I try to use the facts that I know in order to counter my fears. Hopefully, this releases my body from some of the worries it is facing with familiar out-of-control movements and the like.

I think this shows what we need to do in our spiritual lives as well. We need to be prepared before the battles take place; we must have clarity in our minds to protect and guard against the things that we may be feeling in the rest of our bodies and throw truth at it as well. So while I don't know if I will ever truly get over my fear of flying, I am learning ways to grow my spiritual life through it.

I don't believe that since I struggle with this phobia that I'm less of a Christian. But I also don't think it is okay for me to just accept it and stay there. I think I need to keep running to God in my fear. That yes, I'm not actually guaranteed no matter how many statistics or physics are thrown my way, or percentages of how unlikely it is that a plane is going to go down. Those don't help me. What gives me some comfort is knowing that even if I can't control the feelings in my body or what is going to happen to my physical body in that moment (whether feeling the results of a panic attack or the feelings of a plane actually beginning to go down and crash), I can control the truth that I know. Which is this: I will be with Christ, whether in this body and with the Holy Spirit living in me, or if this actually does go down, I will physically be with Him in eternity.

> *If then you have been raised with Christ, seek the things that are above, where Christ is, seated at the right hand of God. Set your minds on things that are above, not on things that are on earth. For you have died, and our life*

> *is hidden with Christ in God. When Christ who is your life appears, then you also will appear with him in glory.*
> Colossian 3:1-4

No, that doesn't stop the plane from crashing, and it doesn't make my body stop freaking out with the shakes, but it reminds me of God's truth. My body may not feel at peace, but I'm hoping that through knowing this, my mind can be at peace. That I don't need to fear the moments before death, because in death that won't matter; death will actually be a new life with Christ.

Something else God's been teaching me is that He doesn't have off days. I think we often confuse silence from God with Him being too busy or ignoring us. Maybe we think He's fed up with us struggling with the same thing over and over again. Our minds are trained to look at God in the same way we look at humans. When we burden a human with the same thing, bring the same conversation up, or admit to messing up with the same sin again, a lot of the time, unfortunately, people step away or get tired of us.

I fear this often when I'm flying. Maybe God is disappointed in me for still battling this phobia and struggling in this branch of anxiety. Lies from the enemy try to tell me that Christ has muted the line and wants a break from hearing this same thing again. But the truth tells me that God doesn't have off days like humans do. He is never changing and always with us. He wants to hear from us, whether we are rejoicing Him on the mountaintops or crying out to Him in our sins and struggles yet again. He will always listen to our cries out to Him.

*"Jesus Christ is the same yesterday and today and forever."* Hebrews 13:8

"For I the LORD, do not change; therefore you, O children of Jacob, are not consumed." Malachi 3:6

"The grass withers, the flower fades, but the word of our God will stand forever." Isaiah 40:8

"God is not human, that he should lie, not a human being, that he should change his mind. Does he speak and then not at? Does he promise and not fulfill?" Numbers 23:19

"But you are the same, and your years have no end." Psalm 102:27

"The steadfast love of the LORD never ceases; his mercies never come to an end." Lamentations 3:22

"For the LORD will not forsake his people; he will not abandon his heritage." Psalm 94:14

Although I'm still really struggling in this area, and while I definitely have not perfected getting over anxieties or phobias that are deeply rooted in the body, God is teaching me that it isn't my job to perfect it. It is my job to wage war against it. Maybe this means just continuing to remember Enya's attitude on life, "Feel the fear but do it anyway" -Susan Jeffers. It might look like just continuing to get on the plane, when everything in me says to run in the opposite direction.

If I go to war with these fears, there will be beautiful outcomes on the other side. I didn't want to get on the plane to Alaska. But now over a week after being back home, and I'm already trying to figure out when we can go again. We hit our fiftieth state goal! We saw the most beautiful forest of fall-colored trees that I've ever seen in my life. Being born and raised in So Cal, and even in the midst of lots of travel, I can't say that I really ever witnessed a real fall. But with

Alaska, I can now say I did. The trees were vibrant and full of all the colors and with beautiful snowy mountaintops peeking out behind them.

Because God challenged me, and because Devin encouraged me to get on that plane, we were able to drive through parks and forests and we got to see a moose cross the road! It was nothing short of magical. If I would have avoided the journey to get there, just deciding to turn around and go home and curl up under the covers to hide, we wouldn't have been able to witness and bask in all of the beauty of the creation that God made in this world for us to enjoy. I don't want to miss out on seeing God's masterpiece because I was afraid.

This is something that He really drove home in me throughout our recovery, even though we continued to face unknowns and uncertainties in our recovery. There have been some giant physical hurdles, as well as mental hurdles, we have come up against, and each time, we have the choice to lay down and give up in the valley. We can choose to stay there and be uncomfortable as we cry and lay on the rocky ground. OR, we can push through the things that feel like they might kill us. We can keep going, keep holding His hand, and each other's, as we begin the trek up the mountaintop. Because the view will just be killer!

The climb is going to get really tough. We'll probably trip and fall. I'm sure our knees are going to be bruised and our elbows are all bloody. There might be some scary animals along the way hissing at us. Our lungs might begin to feel on fire and our breath far from giving us the oxygen that we feel we need. But throughout the climb, we must remember and know that we have to trust the One who made the mountaintops to get us there.

*"They say 'one day at a time,' but there have been an awful lot of one hour at a time's in those days and one minute at a time's in those hours. Whatever 'one' you are working on right now, I'm proud of you."*[3] *- Dion K.*

You know how Minnesota is on the way back to San Diego from Alaska? Just kidding, I'm actually pretty strong in the field of geography. Apparently not spelling though, because it just took me three attempts to spell the word "geography." Anyway ... I knew what I was signing up for when Devin and I were sitting in our airbnb in the middle of beautiful Alaska, as we discussed our plans for the rest of the week. We had no flights home (go figure), so being four days into our trip and realizing that it was beginning to be the season in Anchorage, Alaska, where everything starts closing down due to the weather, we thought we should at least discuss when we wanted to head home.

After a few peaks into flights back to San Diego, somehow we stumbled upon the idea of looking into flights from Alaska to Minnesota. Now, that might seem super random, and it was. But we quickly realized after a few online searches that we could get to Minnesota for about the same price as flying back home. And in addition, we would just need to pay for the flight from Minnesota to California. No biggie. SO I thought. After getting more serious about the idea and deciding that since it was my big sister's birthday weekend, we absolutely had to go and surprise her for it. After a phone call to my brother-in-law Frank to let him know we wanted to surprise my sister, and after getting the okay, next was booking the flights and getting our bags packed for the next day. We then learned that it wouldn't be just one flight, but three separate planes in order to get to Minnesota from our current state. This freaked me out through the roof, but I held on to the fact that I was going to surprise my sister and squeeze all her little ones. That was enough motivation to get on the plane.

First flight was scheduled from Anchorage, Alaska, to Juneau, Alaska. Just over an hour flight, which honestly the shorter flights make me more upset. It feels like so many emotions to go through to just be in the air for an hour. I'd much rather deal with a long flight where I can wear myself out for the middle part of it from all the panic and at least hopefully get a few minutes nap in. So, after doing a quick search on iPhone maps to make sure we couldn't drive to Juneau instead, I zipped up my leather boots and we got on the first flight.

The flight was bumpy, the wind was strong. I felt uncomfortable; oh, and did I mention that there was this old man sitting next to me who wouldn't stop touching me? Well yeah, that happened. As if I wasn't already miserable enough, now this guy keeps putting his hand on my leg and butt. Awesome. I kept letting it go, trying to make sense of it in my mind that maybe he was reaching for his seatbelt. Yeah, that could've been a good excuse for the first time he did it. But it doesn't really add up for the twenty other times he put his hand down.

I tried to breathe, focus on panicking about one thing at a time. Right now, I wanted to focus on trying to calm down from the plane ride. But now the flight attendants are serving food and drinks, and this guy next to me decides to order drinks and get drunk. So let's just say that plane ride got worse: the man freaked me out; my husband wanted to go fight this guy in the airport; and now he's reported to Alaskan Airlines and hopefully will never have the guts to do that again. Okay, so flight number one of three is done.

Next flight, Juneau, Alaska, to Seattle, Washington. I'm not loving this but keep telling myself there's only one more to go. I'm getting tired, and my body is exhausted from going through the first flight, and now onto the next. There's the normal turbulence. I'm squeezing Devin's hand like always, and with the other, I'm squeezing my giant moose stuffed animal. Oh, did I not mention that Devin insisted on buying me a moose stuffie the size of the state of Alaska from the zoo in Anchorage? Okay, maybe I'm overreacting. Clearly it isn't the size of Alaska … probably just like the size of Rhode Island. So I'm buckled in tight. I know this because I've checked my seatbelt multiple times, and I'm shutting my eyes as tight as I can, trying to block out the ride. We finally landed in Seattle, and now we have a seven-hour layover before our next flight. It's well after midnight, and even with our newly repaired broken bones, we find a spot on the not-so-comfy airport floor to crash for a few hours before our final flight.

After some not-so-great sleep, but better than normal for this insomniac, we gathered our things and I shake in my boots as we prepared to board the third flight. This was it, the home stretch before we got to see our family. Three and a half hours, and we'd be done with flights for the weekend. I thought this last flight would be the easiest; however, I realized how wrong I was pretty quickly. The pilot of the aircraft revealed to us pretty early on that there was a storm currently over the state of Montana. This didn't mean much to me at first, but then I got what he meant when suddenly an hour into our flight, we were experiencing the worst turbulence I have ever encountered in all my years of flying.

Devin was doing everything he could to console me. I was trying desperately to ask God to calm me. This was by far turning into my worst post-traumatic stress disorder moment. The flight was turning my body into the fight of its life. I wasn't just crying a few tears; I was bawling and breathing uneasy breaths. I was trying to drown the sounds of the wind and the engine roaring out with my Christian music playlist I had playing on Spotify through my headphones. But everything was so loud I could barely hear the music. Finally, after minutes and minutes of this dragging on, Devin asked me, "Do you want me to have a flight attendant come over to talk to you to see if that helps?" We'd never tried this before, so I thought it couldn't hurt.

Devin hit his call button, and a smiling attendant came over quickly. She assured me that just because the flight attendants had to put their 200-pound drink and snack tray out of the aisle, and even though none of them could stand up because the plane was so bumpy, and even though the pilot came over the intercom and told them as well as passengers that we were all not to get up because it was too dangerous, that even with all of these factors that this was all okay and nothing was wrong. I appreciated her kindness, trying to smile back and even chuckle a bit in my head as I stared at the knife she was holding up in her hand the whole conversation for reasons I may never know. I sat back, still crying, but trying to remember what she said and trust her. But the doubts were creeping in. Maybe she didn't really know. After all, she's just working here in the back of the plane; she's not the one actually controlling it. Maybe this is different than what she thinks.

Less than ten minutes later, another flight attendant came over to our aisle. To understand this moment a bit better, you should first understand our seating arrangement. I was by the window, next to me was Devin, and in the end was a man we didn't know. What we did know was that he wanted to keep to himself. He tried very openly to avoid any kind of interaction with us or the flight crew. So it goes without saying that this same man probably wasn't very amused when this second flight attendant came over and leaned over him and Devin in order to console me.

This flight attendant put his hand out and gestured for me to hold his hand. I'll mention really quickly that this is not something I just go around doing; holding the hands of other men isn't a norm in my day-to-day life. But because my husband was right there in the middle of our hand hold, because I was losing my nerves with this turbulence, and because this flight attendant happened to be gay ... I made an exemption and held his hand. His blue nail polish was probably one of my new favorite colors by the way, and I definitely was jealous by how great his nails looked, especially compared to my polish that was chipping away.

He squeezed my hand and looked me in the eyes through my tears. He told me that there was nothing wrong, and that this turbulence was completely normal. He talked in a calming tone and explained how sometimes he flies in this kind of plane ride four or five times a day with his job as a flight attendant. I equally felt bad for him that he had to go through that, even if he didn't mind. But I also appreciated that he explained this was something he went through all the time. There wasn't a reason to panic. The plane was not going down. This was simply a normal, everyday work day for him. And while I was still nervous even after his reassuring words, I did feel like I caught my breath for a moment. And I know I took his away when I responded to his question, "Can I get you anything?" with a tear-filled response of "A Xanax would be nice." I think people underestimate my ability to crack a joke through my most painful moments.

But it's funny how even after hearing a professional tell you everything will be okay, you can still be afraid. Don't get me wrong; I settled down at least a little bit. And I'll take a little bit of progress any day over nothing. But I think of this in the same way that we treat God sometimes. Christ can be telling us something, and we completely ignore or blow it off because we think we know better. The flight attendant was telling me I didn't need to be afraid. And God often tells me the same thing, "Do not fear." But I continue to think I know better and make an attempt at controlling my circumstances that aren't mine to control.

I was the same way the days leading up to my spinal surgery in the hospital. I'm pretty sure I made my surgeon super mad at my lack of confidence in him performing my surgery. Every time he would come into my ICU room and discuss the surgery with me, I would immediately go into questioning him and make sure he was confident about repairing my spine. The first time I questioned him to whether or not he could successfully perform the surgery, I think he was confused. But the next few times of questioning him, he was definitely put off by my lack of confidence in him.

I went to great lengths to try to prove to him that everyone makes mistakes, and I didn't want him going into surgery with the attitude that he does this all the time so he didn't need to pay as much attention. I remember after him telling me that he has done thousands of these spinal surgeries, I decided to give him the example that I've been a professional softball player who has played all my life but I still make errors on easy plays sometimes. He didn't like that.

And I think about how God must feel that way too sometimes. When I go to him with a list of questions or asking Him to fix things in my life, in the middle of Him trying to respond to me, I begin cutting Him off with my list of reasons as to why He is wrong or why I have the right to worry. That isn't an attitude I should ever be coming to my Creator with. My attitude and posture should be in recognition that He is the One who created me, He is the One who can heal me, and He is the One who holds me in life or in death. My heart shouldn't be in front of Him, giving Him a list of the things I'm allowed to be worried about. My heart should be in a position of me handing it over into His safe hands and asking Him to hold it, no matter what hurts or fears are about to take place. When He's telling me not to worry, it isn't ever about being removed from all the worries and hard things in life. It's about learning how to give over our hearts to the One who is walking with us through it and learning to trust Him to protect that heart no matter what waves or fires form around us.

*"When God says 'don't' we should read that as 'Don't hurt yourself.'"*
[4] *- (Anonymous)*

How often do I hurt myself simply because I'm not allowing my heart to listen to the One trying to protect me? And in all my worry, all I'm doing is hurting myself more.

Alrighty, we can start wrapping this chapter up. But first, I want you to know, and maybe it's already obvious, but our flight to Minnesota made it there safely. We didn't crash, and the turbulence eventually slowed down a bit. Our landing was one of the roughest yet, I will say. And I definitely have a new fear of the plane flipping and rolling after it lands. So that's something new I've gotta work on, but we made it.

We Facetimed my sister and her babies while we were down the street from their house. I bundled up in my snow jacket I had packed for Alaska in order to trick my sister into thinking we were still in the cold and not in the 70-degree weather Minnesota had going on right then. Devin and I suddenly pretended that we saw a family of bears outside the car, and Bry and her kiddos anxiously were asking us to flip my phone camera around so that they could see. Little did they know that the family of bears we were talking about was them, and we were sitting in their driveway. We flipped the camera around so that they had a view of the front of their house, and after their shocked faces sat stunned, Devin and I were quickly bombarded and rushed by all of the sweetest snuggles and loves from our loved ones. That moment made every single flight so worth it.

I think that weekend will always be one of my favorites spent with them. I got to hang out and grow closer to my big sister. I got to laugh with her and go to Target and spend way too much money with her. I got to hold my newest six-week-old nephew and witness him smiling back at me (even if no one else saw it to believe me). I got to snuggle my family and love on the littles that Devin and I adore so much in our lives. Being an aunt and uncle are truly some of our favorite things ever. All of this was possible because we got on the plane. We stepped into the valley and got through it to the end of the climb on the mountaintop. Now the only problem was that the weekend was ending, California was calling us back, and it was time to stop admiring the mountaintop view and start the trek back down the mountain through the valley to get home.

*"Who's the genius that decided to call it "Emotional baggage "..... .....and not "griefcase.""*[5] *- @Dadsaysjokes*

Seriously though. Emotional baggage doesn't capture the grief your body goes through in trauma. I definitely prefer the grief case name in my personal opinion. Sunday evening, we got to the airport and would soon be getting on our flight back to San Diego. Except, this flight also was going to have a layover in Las Vegas, so it meant getting on two flights to get home. And this time, I was crying because we just had to say goodbye to family and flying meant getting further away from their embrace.

As our boarding group was called, and the girl behind the counter scanned our tickets, we began walking down the long hallway that attaches the airport to the plane. I started hearing the whirling of the engine of the plane. I stopped, froze, and had to lean my head against the hallway wall. Tears were rushing down, my body was sporadically shaking, and in that moment, I was certain I was not stepping foot on that plane. People passed I'm sure annoyed that we were in the way and holding them up. This went on until the last possible second. And yet again, we boarded that plane.

Now that plane ride was one of my worst ever. Turbulence wasn't even really a thing. Take-off was scary, and it was just over a two-hour flight. I should have been fine. We were near the front of the plane after them bumping up our seats. I could see the flight attendants and had my eyes on them for as long as they sat. They laughed, joked, and talked. I was still convinced we were crashing.

There's a lot that happened on that flight. Most details honestly are fuzzy because my mind completely destroyed not only my mental capacity on that flight but my body also felt wrecked. I couldn't open my eyes, not because I was tired but I assume after trying hard to keep them tightly shut for so long, they were exhausted and needed to stay closed. Which, I'll add, is difficult when you're trying to exit a plane. My body felt like it had just run fifty miles. I was achy and tired everywhere. I couldn't complete a thought. I know this because I tried over and over. Just trying to formulate a simple sentence in my head was seemingly impossible.

Devin was trying to communicate with me, but I couldn't communicate back. Now he was freaked; I was laying across two airport benches; and my husband was realizing I was having a mental breakdown. Throughout our layover, I was determined that I was not getting on the next plane. I told myself, *Why do you keep doing this? Quit getting on the stupid planes and getting yourself upset like this. This is your fault for continuing to get into these situations.* I tried to tell Devin that I wasn't getting on the next plane. And when he asked if he should go get a rental car to make the four-plus-hour drive home, a new wave of emotions took over with the guilt that I was making this difficult not only on myself, but now I was making it hard on Devin. I was forcing him to get into a situation where he had to make a long drive home instead of just getting on the less-than-an-hour flight home.

I had a breakdown. That's an understatement, but that's as close as I can get to describing that layover. As I battled back and forth in my head, while at the same time struggling to get my thoughts through the fog, I dozed off on the airport bench battling with myself.

After a couple hours, I woke up. I decided that this was a spiritual war going on around me. I needed to step outside of it so that I could see and witness the battle overtaking me. After stepping to the side, God presented me with this thought.

I could get on the plane home, and there would be a small chance that it would crash. Or I could give into the lies the enemy was telling me. The enemy was telling me to never get on a plane again. I then recognized this as him trying to ruin one of the things I love most: traveling. If the enemy could convince me to never get on a plane again, then I couldn't go traveling to go love on my family. I couldn't get on a plane to go make memories and explore God's creation with my husband. I couldn't do things that God uses for good, because I was believing the lies of the enemy.

So yes, I could have chosen to tell Devin that we needed to get a rental car. I could've allowed the enemy to win in a moment where he saw me as vulnerable, as I was facing one of my biggest fears, while facing emotional exhaustion on top of it all. Or I could choose to take God's hand and step into the uncertainty. To face the fears and the lack of things I couldn't control, but choose to do them anyway as a way to show that I trust in the One who holds my tomorrow. I could choose to step on that plane to tell the enemy to go back home and to continue waging war on this battle in my mind and in my body.

So ... I got on the plane.

*"Let's not get to our graves safely." -Devin*

Now we're home, that plane also didn't crash, and I spent the next several days recovering mentally and physically from all that my body went through during those flights. I can tell you now that I'm still dreading the next flight I've got to take, but I'm trying to come up with a strategy in order to counter those fears.

Something interesting I learned is that aerophobia (fear of flying) is actually caused and formed from other anxieties that build up to it and/or make the fear worse. Fear of flying often stems from fear of heights, fears of leaving the house, fear of people, fear of confined places, and fears of germs.

I found this super interesting and can definitely say I struggle with a few of those fears on top of my other worries. And although my fear isn't cured, I'm choosing to grab hold of Christ's hand and continue on. My job isn't to fix myself and cure my phobia. My job is to hand my fear over to Christ and ask Him to help me walk through it. But asking Him to take over doesn't just give me an excuse to sit on the sidelines and wait for Him to cure me. It looks like putting in the work. Some days this looks like just trusting God enough to get on the plane afraid. Some days it looks like researching how airplanes function, learning more about the phobia of flying, and diving into what drives those fears, digging out the roots where those fears have dug in.

So with the help of Christ, I will continue to get on planes, and maybe one of these days one will crash land. But if it's a water landing, that'll be okay because I know exactly what to do in that situation.

I'm actually one of those people who pays attention every flight to what the flight attendants are instructing through that training in the "unlikely event of a water landing."

I'm going to keep getting on the plane to explore God's creation. I'm going to keep squeezing my husband's hand and probably crying through all the turbulence. I'm going to keep visiting family and holding them tightly in my embrace after every scary flight. Because this is for those I love. This is to fight the enemy and tell him that I know the One in charge. This is for God and handing Him my heart, because I know I can't get through these scary moments without Him holding the moments safely in His hands, as He walks beside me through this valley.

# Chapter 12: Body Image

*"Waiting on God requires the willingness to bear uncertainty—to carry within oneself the unanswered question, lifting the heart to God about it whenever it intrudes upon one's thoughts."*[1] - Elisabeth Elliot

BODY IMAGE ... HMM, you might be thinking, *This is a weird topic for a book based on a car accident.* I would have told you the same exact thing a year ago. I never considered our image of our bodies and the wreckage of a car crash to go hand in hand. Until that's what my world turned into.

And maybe you think I'm going into this topic because the places where my skin was once smooth and clear now hold many scars from surgeries, cuts, bruises, and the staples and stitches that were used to hold and put me back together. I can't tell you the amount of people who came to me throughout our recovery, trying to encourage me that my scars weren't "that bad" when, honestly, that was never a concern of mine. I actually kind of like scars. I've had a lot of surgeries and injuries throughout my life. I have freckles that people may not like, but I've always loved them. I have tattoos and piercings. I have stretch marks and marks from the life that I have lived. I love those things about me. They are the evidence of the body that has been on a journey and has a story behind the scars. So no, to answer your question you're thinking in your head, this chapter is not to address body image in regards to scars. Though, if you are in a place where you are struggling with the way your body looks because of scars and marks you may be insecure about, I believe that this chapter is for you too. The things God has taught me about my body can encourage you and hopefully grow your thinking in this area as well.

Now before I dive too deep into this subject, I want you to know that I don't know everything when it comes to this. Body image is such a huge topic with so many branches you could go off of in a discussion. There's the psychology behind why some suffer with eating disorders, such as anorexia or bulimia. Then there's another branch with those who suffer from not being able to gain weight or not being able to lose weight due to medical health issues. I'm sure there's more branches, but before our accident, those were the only two I honestly knew about.

But then there's me, who somehow grew up being an athlete, which meant I had more muscles than most of my friends, but at the same time I wasn't overweight. I was never a twig like my friends, who weren't allowed to eat snacks because their parents were health-food freaks. Meanwhile, I was allowed to eat virtually anything because we definitely weren't a health-food freak family. I remember sitting next to my friends on benches and realizing that my thighs were thicker than their skinny legs.

I remember as I got older and somehow still was a "healthy weight," according to my doctors, at the fitness studio that I worked at where Barre was taught, I was still considered much bigger than all the women that came through the door. I didn't have the dancer body; I wasn't tall and slim. I was somehow a fit, muscular girl who wasn't very tall and definitely wasn't graceful like a dancer. I think working at the facility was the first time I realized that I wasn't measuring up and felt I was being looked up and down for the way I didn't look but was supposed to.

I worked the front desk, and I often felt guilty that I was seemingly the face of this company, or at least this campus of the company, yet I didn't fit the mold. After working there for a few months and taking classes regularly, women started coming in telling me how good I looked and how I had lost weight. I honestly hadn't noticed. Heck, we didn't even own a scale but somehow I was beginning to feel like my body was becoming more acceptable to my peers and women that were surrounding me.

After I had to quit that job because of family health issues happening, one after another, I didn't think much of my body image anymore. I remember thinking back to how unhealthy my mindset was when I was working in that place. I no longer felt like I needed to fit a mold; I felt healthy and exercised regularly through the things I loved. But I just remember feeling a weight dropped off my back because I wasn't surrounded by a studio of mirrors and peers telling me that I needed to look a certain way.

Now fast forward to a few years later, Devin and I joined an Orange Theory gym. If you aren't familiar with Orange Theory, I'll just describe it as a workout that completely kicks your butt. Part of the one-hour class, you are on a treadmill running your heart out, often at an incline. During the next part of class, you are on a row machine, rowing on this boat that isn't going anywhere but somehow your entire body is on fire from head to toe. And then there's the part of class where you're doing burpees, lifting weights, and hanging onto these random ropes on the wall that make you hold up your entire body weight to the point that your biceps begin to tremble. I'm sure there's a better way to explain it, but let's just say they even have a week called "Hell week," and if that doesn't give you a picture of how intense the workout is, I don't know what will.

All that to say, I absolutely loved it. The born and raised athlete in me loved being pushed to my limits and exhausting my body to the point where it shook. This was a place where Devin and I would go to recharge after so much chaos going on in our lives around us. This was the place where we could put away our phones and not feel like we had to take care of anything or anyone, except for ourselves and to grow in our physical health.

After trying it out for a class, we found out that this gym had a competition coming up. It was a transformation challenge that would take place over the course of the next eight weeks. The requirements were to do weekly weigh-ins, show up to at least three classes a week, and at the end of it all, the woman and the man who lost the most amount of weight would win a check of $500. We immediately signed up, but I wasn't in the thought process where I felt I could lose the most amount of weight. In fact, my weight wasn't even a concern at all to me. I had recently gone to the doctor for a regular checkup and the doctor commented about how my weight looked really good. But during this competition, we had to do weekly weigh-ins. This process ended up eating at me. I realized that no matter how well I ate, no matter how fast I ran, or how many classes I showed up to, the scale wasn't going down. In fact, some days it would even go up a couple pounds.

I began to feel a huge wave of guilt and shame take over me. I felt I was disappointing the coaches around me or that I was failing them. I tried calorie counts, hardly eating anything in a day, and running my heart out, but nothing was budging. I couldn't understand why I was doing everything I possibly could to make the right healthy choices, but I wasn't getting any results. I didn't know what was wrong with me.

After a few weeks of continuing on in the challenge, I started realizing that for the first time in my life, I was enjoying learning how to run. Yes, I grew up a softball and baseball player, but running was not my strong suit. I would do anything to get out of the warm up jog every practice, and running the bases nearly killed me every time I would get a home run. But now suddenly I was learning how to breath a bit so I didn't feel like I was dying and was growing stronger in my legs. I was learning that running not just inside of the Orange Theory gym but also in my neighborhood was extremely healthy not just for my physical health, but for my mental health as well.

I started running nearly every day and looking forward to pushing myself, hopefully growing stronger in my distance for runs. I knew each run I would have a bit of a panic attack because breathing was still scary, and learning to stay calm when I was out of breath became a new way that I had to rely on God. I found myself talking to God more and spending time with Him on those runs through talking with Him and listening to Him through Christian music playing in my headphones each run.

After a few weeks of just trying to learn to get to a mile, I found out that Orange Theory had a 5K race coming up. I remember being excited and wanting to sign up for it right away. In the week leading up to the race, I ran my first 5K at nine at night in our neighborhood. I remember the huge smile on my face that I couldn't get rid of when

I walked in the door of our house and told Devin that for the first time ever, I ran 3.1 miles without stopping at all!

Learning to run became not only a way that I grew in my relationship with Christ, but a way that started healing the mental wounds I was experiencing from beating myself up for the way that my body looked. And even though, at the end of the eight-week transformation challenge I didn't win according to the scale, in my mind I did win because I suddenly and unexpectedly had lost seven pounds. After that final weight-in, I didn't think about the scale. My whole mindset had switched to learning to become a better runner and growing in that area. God used running to repair wounds that were brought on by my own shame; I didn't need to lose those seven pounds, but it's kind of funny how the minute that I stopped obsessing and learned to grow in a new way with Christ, that is when results happened. That is when my overall health became much better.

So now click fast forward on the remote again. Now we're in a car accident and I'm put on all kinds of medications. After being on antidepressants for a while now, my doctors want to switch me to a different one. I find out months later that this specific antidepressant makes you gain at least a pound, maybe two, per week. I wasn't aware of that. Add on top of that all kinds of pain medications, and my body is on multiple vitamins because all the blood loss made me inefficient in many areas. Now I'm on sleeping pills because not sleeping is no longer an option when your body is shattered and needs rest to repair and recover.

When I was in my bed in rehab, I remember a nurse coming in one night and weighing me on the scale I apparently had on the bottom of my hospital bed. I remember it was a few pounds over what my normal resting weight was. Admittedly, I was put off about the weight, but she assured me that the bed is not always accurate, and I was also dealing with a lot of swelling from all of my injuries. I decided I didn't need to worry about it, because she was right and if I did have extra weight on me right now, it made sense given the circumstances.

The next time I jumped on a scale (well, didn't really jump because my back is fused now, and that's not a great idea) was at my nearly four-month checkup with my spinal surgeon. At that time, I noticed I was about nine pounds over my "normal" weight. I remember telling the nurse who weighed me that this wasn't normal, and she even put in my chart that the scale wasn't accurate. Another hiccup, but I tried to brush it off and move on, not allowing it to affect me. Even later on in the appointment, my doctor had made the comment that the reason I was feeling all the weird sensations so much in my back was because of how "skinny" my back was. This gave me the affirmation I needed that I was okay and didn't need to freak out over my weight right now.

So now we're a month after that appointment. Over the holiday months of Christmas and New Year's, my mental and physical health took a turn for the worse. I began feeling like a guinea pig, and just about every other day, my medication was being switched on me for my mental health. Some medications made me sleep all day, and I couldn't stay awake. So then I'd get switched to a new sleeping medication, which would make my insomnia worse and I wouldn't sleep at all for days on end.

In the midst of all that, my antidepressants were being upped. My pain medication wasn't helping so I ditched it and began having major numbness and pain down my left leg. My spinal doctor prescribed me a steroid to take for a couple of weeks to hopefully take away the inflammation and the numbness I was experiencing. Well let's just say the steroid didn't work, and the cocktail between my new dosage of antidepressants and steroid had made it so that I was now experiencing hunger pains I had never had before.

Unfortunately, I will never forget going to put on a pair of pants just a couple weeks after that steroid, and the pants that fit me previously I now couldn't get past my knees. Over the course of that point of recovery, I had now gained over thirty pounds. I was devastated, embarrassed, and felt confused about what I was supposed to do. I wasn't allowed to exercise much with my injuries; and this medication I was taking every day now became not only something I dreaded because of the way it made me feel in my head, but now I despised it because it caused me to gain this weight and have this issue I never experienced before. I was so upset and didn't understand why after everything that we had just gone through, now God was allowing me to have to go through this on top of everything else. It felt unfair and like I had my hands tied because there was literally nothing I could do to lose this weight.

A few weeks after the initial shock of the weight gain, I told my doctor I was going to take a break from my medications because I couldn't handle the side effects of weight gain on top of everything else that was causing me to spiral in my mind. What I didn't tell him was that I wasn't just planning to take a break; I was going to go cold turkey off of everything. I was already suffering so much with the war inside of my mind, and I didn't need an eating disorder to be added into the mix of all that.

That same week, Devin helped me order an exercise bike. This was the one exercise I was cleared to do by my spinal surgeon. The first week I had the bike, I pushed my body far past what I thought I could. I was determined to lose the weight as quickly as I could. I biked 100 miles: I sweat, I cried, and I jumped back on that scale. My results? A heart-dropping moment of not even losing half a pound ... yeah, that defeat was real.

This began a new journey that God was working on in my heart and mind. Actually, it hasn't felt so much like a journey. A journey makes me think of a walk-through somewhere, but this felt like a new battle. It felt like the enemy was coming at me from all sides, and I wasn't just walking through somewhere. I was instead running and turning to shoot arrows at the spears being thrown at me from every angle.

I'm not out of the woods yet either. I still have weight to lose, and I still have many breakdowns over the body I grieve that I used to have. But there is a lot that God has taught me and challenged me on along the way. I've had the opportunity to be vulnerable and open up on my social media accounts on this area of my life and where I'm struggling. There was one specific post where I had multiple people reach out to me afterward and had some amazing conversations on how God was able to work through my post to reach their hearts, and how they related and were encouraged by it. I'd like to share that post here, under a photo of myself that I was self-conscious of where I'm sitting holding a cute rainbow latte in a cute coffee shop but not feeling cute myself. However, I felt like God was pushing me to post anyway so I wrote this:

*Yep, I gained some weight...*

*Maybe you can't even tell, but I definitely can and have been positive everyone around me has noticed this month.*

*A not-so-fun fact: when your body goes through major trauma, your body tries to process over twenty new medications, and sleep is out the window completely, turns out your body doesn't like it.*

*I've felt like a lab rat. I've been exhausted and angry. I asked God what I'm supposed to get out of this... I was talking with Him, and saying, "Okay, God, I understand You allow me to go through hard stuff to grow and mature my faith in You. But I don't get why the supposed solutions to my struggles are making things worse. Why does the steroid that's supposed to take away the pain and numbness and tingling in my legs make me puff up so extreme? What am I supposed to learn from no longer fitting in my favorite clothes that I've had for nearly ten years and have so much trouble losing it with being so limited in my mobility?"*

*I've never been afraid to go outside with the fear of people making fun of my weight ... I can't recall a time where I was self-conscious about getting my picture taken because I'd have to see how puffy I look.*

*Christ hasn't given me a full answer yet to why I'm walking through this when quite honestly, I feel I need a break after these last five months.*

*Though, He showed me this reminder in James 1:2-8 yesterday! It starts with encouraging us to find joy in the midst of trials because Christ is maturing our faith. It goes on to talk about how God is generous, and He wants to give us good things. BUT, when we ask, we can't live in the thought that He doesn't really care or love us enough, or that we are some exception to who He wants to be generous to. I don't want to be a shifting wave tossed by the windy doubt. I went to God to help take away these hard things, to help me get comfortable in my body once again.*

*Now He may not necessarily make me skinny immediately. But I can have full confidence that He has some reason for this. Even if I don't get to have an answer right now. He doesn't owe me anything. Yet, I owe Him everything.*

*So, I just wanna put this out there cause I feel like God is putting it on my heart and I'm praying He encourages someone out there who might be fighting a similar battle with body image. Work hard; He does love us just the way we are, but that isn't an excuse to sit comfortably and live in glutton. He gave us these bodies to move and spread love to His kingdom. I can' shrink back and be afraid to see others with fear of their thoughts of me. That is NOT from Christ. Have confidence that He will give you as His child whatever is BEST for your faith.*

So here I am, ten months after that post. I'm again sitting in a coffee shop, typing away at this chapter as I take small sips of my iced vanilla latte on the cute chunk of wood used as a table beside my seat. I've learned a lot since that post, but honestly, I still am struggling quite a bit with feeling insecure in my body. As I drink my latte, I now have a new thought that wasn't here a year ago when I would drink coffee or eat anything for that matter. I now have a little lie that comes up and tries to shoot an arrow at me, telling me, "Do you know how much fat and sugar is probably in that coffee you're drinking? Remember all that weight you worked hard to lose this week? Well you are most definitely gaining all that back from drinking this one coffee."

And ten months ago, I probably would've had a major meltdown and not ordered the coffee and starved myself until midnight when I would start crying because the hunger pains were so bad. This would result in Devin needing to run out to get me an emergency quesadilla from the only Mexican food joint open at that time of night. If you think that is a funny example, I wish it were just an example. Unfortunately, I have to say that it was a real story, and it was a normal reoccurrence that happened multiple times in the beginning of my struggle-with-weight journey. Let me just state for the record: STARVING YOURSELF ALL DAY WILL NOT HELP YOU LOSE WEIGHT AND WILL DESTROY YOUR MENTAL HEALTH.

Every time I tried an extreme weight-loss strategy, not only did I not lose the desired weight but I started feeding into the lies the enemy was putting in my head. I believed that my weight determined my worth, and I was living in extreme shame at the way that I now looked on the outside, instead of focusing on how God could use this in the insides of my heart.

So I'm here, drinking this latte that might make me gain a pound, or I could stay the same. Does my worth in God change based on that? Not at all. And now I'm here, and just yesterday I reached the 20-pound mark. Twenty pounds are gone of the thirty-one pounds I gained. And you know the crazy thing about it all? I can't tell the difference from now to a few months ago when I was twenty pounds heavier. I look at photos from the beginning of this year, and now I see the same weight and puffiness on my body. But other people are now telling me that they see the difference; they notice the changes and how I'm beginning to look like myself again.

This is so bizarre to me. How can others see this, but I can't? Have you ever heard of the term "body dysmorphia"? Don't worry if you haven't. It's a newish concept to me too. Mayo Clinic defines it like this: *"Body dysmorphic disorder is a mental health condition in which you can't stop thinking about one or more perceived defects or flaws in your appearance"* [2]

As I've read more into this, I've learned that there are so many people out there who struggle without even realizing that they are suffering from it. When looking in the mirror, your mind basically tricks you to zero in on and convince you that you have a certain flaw, that you are heavier than you are, or that you look a certain way when you don't. Your mind is literally lying to you. Does this sound like something familiar to you? A lie being told, but so darn close to the truth and sneakily tempting you to believe something you're being fed?

Remember Eve in the garden? After God told her not to eat from the Tree of Good and Evil, the serpent didn't say, "You must have misunderstood; your God didn't say you couldn't eat it." Because if the serpent did that, Eve would have just shot back with what God said. Instead, the serpent got a little closer, speaking in soft, comforting tones that were meant to come across as trustworthy and calm. He didn't flat out tell a lie; instead, he made Eve question the truth. The serpent said, "Did God really say that?" He didn't accuse; he confused.

*"Now the serpent was more crafty than any of the wild animals the LORD God has made. He said to the woman, 'Did God really say, "You must not eat from any tree in the garden?"'" Genesis 3:1*

Eve even goes on to tell him that God had said they could eat from the other trees, but if they ate from this specific one, then they would die. But the serpent confused her and led her to believe she just misunderstood God. And then he went even further to convince her that God actually wasn't completely telling the whole truth, because if they knew the whole truth, then they would become as powerful and equal like God.

We look at this and often I'm even like, "Come on, Eve! Seriously! Don't you see that he is lying to you? DON'T DO IT, EVE!" But it's crazy that I can stand in front of a mirror and believe the lies that the enemy feeds me that are so similar. When I try to say to the enemy, "God loves me as I am," he whispers back, "Well maybe, but if you gain any more weight, you're going to be an embarrassment to His kingdom because no one is going to want to be around you if you look ugly." Or I try to say, "My worth is in Christ; I'm working my hardest and I have to leave the rest up to God. He knows what is best for me, and if losing weight is what is best, then He will help me make it happen." But the enemy then screams back, "You are a failure; nothing you are doing is working, and God is too busy with bigger issues. He isn't concerned with your weight. He doesn't care. You're on your own in this. Maybe He doesn't want good things for you."

When I give into these lies, I see myself through the lens of unworthiness, shamefulness, and ugliness. I allow the enemy to win, and he doesn't just win by making me believe and give into his lies. He makes me get to a point where I have been ashamed to leave the house. Where I'm more concerned with the way I look to others when I go out instead of being concerned with loving on people and sharing the love of Christ to those people around me. So, I want to challenge you with one of the big questions that helped me stand up to this lie and encouraged me to leave the house on days where I don't feel very comfortable in my own skin.

How much is not believing that you are enough costing you today? For me, it has cost me photos I could've taken with loved ones to capture memories of us together. I've given into the lie of being fearful to take photos because of the way I've looked and missed out on some of those awesome opportunities. I've said no to events because I was afraid of others looking at me with shame and judging my appearance. I've missed out on loving others and having them love me because I looked at my body through the lens of the enemy instead of looking at it through the lens of Christ. It was never about my body; it was about my heart on the matter.

First Samuel 16:7 puts it this way:

"But the LORD said to Samuel, 'Do not consider his appearance or his height, for I have rejected him. The LORD does not look at the things man looks at. Man looks at the outward appearance, but the LORD looks at the heart.'"

Like I said before, I've still got my helmet on, my shield up, and my sword ready in this battle. I'm realizing that twenty pounds ago I thought I would be happy if I just lost twenty pounds. Now twenty pounds lighter and I feel like I'm still not happy with my weight, but maybe if I lose that last eleven pounds I will be. But I'm learning that it doesn't matter if I'm a hundred pounds heavier than I am now, or fifty pounds lighter than I am right now. My happiness cannot rely on what the number on the scale says. That has never been what this lesson was about. God is teaching me that even though this doesn't sound like a normal problem for a recovering car accident survivor, it is a part of our story. This is something that God has been and is somehow going to use to grow me in my faith, and hopefully reach others on a similar path.

And even though I don't have all the answers, I'm learning that I still have to put in the work on this battlefield. Twenty pounds was not an easy thing to shed. When I finally got cleared again to run, I thought I could start shedding the weight easily. Nope. The only thing that has made a difference is doing a keto diet. I know, I know. Health coaches will tell you it's not sustainable. And I'd agree wholeheartedly. I don't last more than a couple days on keto before I'm miserable, my mental health starts going downhill, and my emotions start taking a hit. There are certain foods that your brain needs to fuel it and going on the keto diet is not something that feeds those needs of your brain.

BUT, going on keto for a day or two once a week, or even once a month, has been my go-to. I can lose a pound, maybe two sometimes, and for the rest of the days, God has been growing me to fuel my body with food, learning healthy habits in the meantime. I'm learning to run in order to strengthen my legs and the body I have that was once broken and shredded apart. Running has not been a successful way to lose weight in this season, so instead of giving up on it all together; I have to believe that God can still use running as a way to help me maintain a weight. But more than that, it is helping teach me healthy lifestyle choices. Some days I don't want to get out of bed. But Christ nudges me that even when I don't feel like it, going out on a run or even a walk is so beneficial not just to my physical health but my mental health as well.

I'm learning there are in fact yummy foods that can be healthy too. Before the accident, I could eat all the junk food I wanted and exercise a couple times a week without gaining a pound. But this body is now new and foreign to me since the crash. I've had to learn to eat good foods, and when I'm not doing keto, I'm still allowed to eat ice cream and things with high calories. But the difference now? I have to learn to say no to some things. I don't have to eat everything that looks good in front of me. And if I'm on vacation, or someone puts hard work into some food for me that may carry a lot of calories or fat, I'm not going to say no to fellowshipping with them and deny something they worked so hard on for me. Instead, I will enjoy and thank God for those yummy treats, while learning that my body also will need to work on metabolism and the next day eat healthier. It looks like running and doing the exercises I love is in order to love my body, not to punish it because I hate it.

I've been convicted many times these past few months when I come back from a run of analyzing my legs and realizing that they look thicker than they used to. And in those moments of nitpicking my legs, God convicts me and tells me, "Don't you realize that those same legs that you are picking apart are the same legs that you once could not use? Those legs now allow you to run, and swim, and hike, and walk into the arms of those you love. Those legs that you are picking on are the same legs that I blessed you with to be able to have the ability to move again when once you laid in a hospital bed, unsure if you'd even ever been able to use them again." Ouch, convicted? Yup. Big time.

So, in those moments when I'm allowing my shield to be dropped and the enemy to take those jabs at me, where I begin to zero in on the lies and accept them as truth, God steps in and reminds me of this: my body was once broken, but by His healing hand, He has allowed it to be made new. I don't know how to use it yet completely, and some days I feel all floopy. But my job is to be thankful that I can still move it. That even though there are new struggles and new hurdles to jump through, I have the ability to jump through those. So, on days when I feel like I want to tell my body how terrible it is, I am learning that I am so blessed to be able to run and jump and move and swim and hike. With the arm that was in a sling, I now get to catch softballs and throw around those I love in big embraces.

This body is not perfect; it never will be because it's not my forever home. That doesn't give me the right to just feed it food that is bad for it and to give up. My job is to take care of it so that it can function in the ways God wants so that it can benefit and be used for His kingdom. It reminds me of the verse my mom wrote on a rock for me and snuck in my backpack before I boarded the plane to my first mission trip to South Africa in high school. The rock had this written on it: "How beautiful on the mountains are the feet of those who bring good news..." Isaiah 52:7

Those feet that hold the bodies are beautiful, no matter the size, because the hearts that are being held by those bodies are bringing the good news of Christ.

I want to leave you with a few quotes and verses that have helped me along the way through this battlefield, specifically relating to body image. Some God has spoken through His Word, others I've seen on posters, billboards, social media, or read in books. They are ones I often go to and am reminded of on days where I feel like I'm losing the battle and feel insecure in my skin. Some just gave me a good laugh, and sometimes that is a requirement when you're feeling cruddy in your own skin. God has used them to convict, encourage, and challenge me. I hope and pray that they do the same for you (if not more so!).

*"Do you not know that your bodies are temples of the Holy Spirit, who is in you, whom you have received from God? You are not your own; you were bought at a price. Therefore, honor God with your bodies."* 1 Corinthians 6:19-20

*"If you can't yet say kind things about your body then maybe focus on not saying mean things to your body first."* [3] - (Anonymous)

*"Am I now trying to win the approval of human beings or of God? Or am I trying to please people? If I were still trying to please people, I would not be a servant of Christ."* Galatians 1:10

*"If tomorrow, women woke up and decided they really liked their bodies, imagine how many industries would go out of business."* [4] - Gail Dines

*"This body is an instrument to use, not an ornament to be displayed."* [5] -Ross Edgley

"Nobody recovers from trauma while hating and punishing themselves. Nobody blames and shames themselves into a better headspace."[6] - Dr. Glenn Patrick Doyle

"We often think Christian maturity is needing help less and less. Wrong. Maturity is realizing how dependent we are on Jesus more and more. Self-reliance is self-sabotage."[7] - J.A. Medders

"A Jesus who never wept could never wipe away my tears."[8] - Charles H. Spurgeon

"Consider how precious a soul must be, when both God and the devil are after it."[9] - Charles Spurgeon

"Eating enough food: You must eat enough food to recover. It will also help to eliminate urges to binge. And normalize cravings for your fear foods. If you're restricting, you will be malnourished and not be in the best mental state to tackle fears. The key to being able to normalize and neutralize fear foods is eating enough food to restore your body and mind."[10] - (Anonymous)

"Photos are only 'snapshots' of particular moments, angles, and doesn't mean they always accurately depict the object. For instance, we may take a photo of a beautiful scenery and then say. 'Well, the photo doesn't capture the actual beauty of the scenery,' but we don't say, 'It's not that beautiful in the photo, therefore the scenery must actually not be that amazing.'"[11] -(Anonymous)

"There are chemicals in my body and false signals in my brain making me feel this way—this is not me. Tolerating this is strength, not weakness. What I decided to do next is important."[12] ~Joshua Fletcher @anxietyjosh

"Do you suppose that the same Son of God that stood in the furnace with Shadrach, Meshach, and Abednego is not also standing with you? Your furnace may look different than theirs but the One alongside you has not changed."[13] - (Anonymous)

"I can't stop thinking about Elijah sitting underneath the juniper tree and asking God to die. God sent an angel who says, 'This journey is too much for you. Rest and eat.' And Elijah does. He wakes up still feeling hopeless, and the angel repeats himself. It took Elijah longer than he wanted to get better. Sometimes we want to move but we can't. Sometimes the journey is too much. It is not a sin to understand your limitations. Start there, get stronger, then get up." [14] -Liberty Underwood

"He who counts the stars and calls them by their names is in no danger of forgetting His own children." [15] - Charles Spurgeon

"God deliberately chooses imperfect vessels — those who have been wounded, those with physical or emotional limitations. Then he prepares them to serve and sends them out with their weakness still in evidence, so that his strength can be made perfect in that weakness." [16] - Christine Caine

"You can't love only the 'socially acceptable' parts of you, without embracing all the things that make you YOU. You can't love your body under the conditions of looking 'perfect' and posed, without also accepting the rolls, lumps and bumps that come along with it. You can't give your time, love, and effort to relationships that only love your 'best' either." [17] - Bree Lenehan

"Mosaics are made from broken pieces, but they're still beautiful works of art, and so are you.." [18] - (Anonymous)

"When people ask me what it looks like to follow Jesus, I say following Him looks like dealing with all of the issues everyone else does disappointments, tremendous joy, uncertainty and having your mind constantly change as you learn how Jesus would have dealt with these emotions." [19] - Bob Goff

"Be content to be nothing, for that is what you are ... Continue, with double earnestness, to serve your Lord, when no visible result is before you. Any simpleton can follow the narrow path in the light: faith's rare wisdom *enables us to march on in the dark with infallible accuracy, since she places her hand in that of her Great Guide. Between this and heaven there may be tougher weather yet, but it is all provided for by our covenant Head ... When we cannot see the face of our God, to trust under the shadow of His wings."* [20] *- Charles Spurgeon; Encouragement for the Depressed*

# Chapter 13: Is This Never-ending? Or Maybe It's Long-suffering

*"Scars don't matter, little one. They are the marks of the battles we have won."*[1] *- Helen Dunmore*

IT'S COMING TO THE end of the weekend. Devin and I are currently watching the show *Survivor* to have some sitting still time before we're about to face a hefty week ahead. First off, I'm noticing very quickly that trying to write while simultaneously watching a show isn't the easiest thing in the world. And two, some of these people on this show apparently have no idea what they have signed up for.

If you aren't familiar with the show (we were too as we just started watching last week), the basis of the show involves about sixteen to twenty contestants battling to survive as they are basically abandoned on an island. They fight through physical and mental competitions as teams and individually in order to win rewards that could include food, immunity from being voted off the island, or safety for their team.

What surprises me is how many people seem surprised when their circumstances get tough when they step foot on the sand or dirt of the place they will now call home for up to forty days. We've watched as contestants have had major meltdowns when the rain begins and then seems unending. When their stomachs grow in pain as they suffer the luxury of food besides whatever they can find around them. And when they are shocked when others want to vote them off the island in order to save their own selves so that they can get closer to winning the show. It surprises me how surprised these people are.

It reminds me of that verse in 1 Peter 4:12 where the apostle Peter writes:

*"Dear friends, do not be surprised at the painful trial you are suffering, as though something strange were happening to you..."*

And while I can sit and watch this silly show, looking at these people while shaking my head at how they are surprised that they have to learn and adapt to survival techniques in order to survive, I have to take a step back and realize that I do the same exact thing in my daily life when I face something hard. I sit and act surprised when we have to go through pain, someone hurts my feelings, I face a difficult decision, where a loved one gets sick, when disaster strikes our country, and more. But suffering and hardships are promised in this life. And while some days it may feel like a game of *Survivor*, we can hold on to the hope that just like in the show, this will end one day. It may be longer than the forty days of the show. We might face wave after wave of difficult tragedies in our lives, but we can hold on to the hope that our reward is in heaven in eternity with Christ. Our time in this world is just testing the strength of our faith in order to grow us into stronger souls for eternity.

I'm reminded of some Scriptures that Paul writes in 1 Corinthians 1:8-9. The verses read:

> *We do not want you to be uninformed, brothers and sisters, about the troubles we experience in the province of Asia. We were under great pressure, far beyond our ability to endure, so that we despaired of life itself. Indeed, we felt we had received the sentence of death. But this happened that we might not rely on ourselves but on God, who raises the dead.*

The truth is that this passage is comforting but also a tough pill to swallow. On one hand we can take comfort in knowing that it isn't uncommon for Christ followers to suffer. Paul went through it, along with many of the other people we look up to throughout Scripture. But it also means that we will encounter tough things, for the sake of the gospel, and then other times simply because we live in a world that is broken and full of chaos. Some will be purposeful in order to grow and stretch our belief in the Lord. But it's important to know too that we will also just feel the aftershock or the back of the hand from the mistakes that others make along the way; we may just get caught in the current of their sins.

In the circumstances that we have faced over the last year, I've realized that we've encountered a bit of both. We have lived in the backwash of someone else making a mistake by not obeying the law. We didn't do anything wrong; we were simply coming to a stop because we were obeying the law. Devin mentioned to me today how crazy it is that we ended up so hurt because we obeyed the law and the rules of the road. The reality is that if we would have disobeyed the law and ran the red light, we most likely would have avoided the whole crash and not suffered the consequences of that disastrous night.

And it's tough when we get stuck in situations of life like this. When we feel like we are doing everything right, and trying our best to serve God, but then life doesn't get easier; it might actually get harder. Have you heard the story in John 9:1-7 where Jesus heals a man who was born blind? Something caught my attention recently in these verses that I want to share with you here.

> *As he went along, he saw a man blind from birth. His disciples asked him, "Rabbi, who sinned, this man or his parent's, that he was born blind?"*
>
> *"Neither this man nor his parents sinned," Jesus said, "but this happened so that the works of God might be displayed in him. As long as it is day, we must do the works of him who sent me. Night is coming, when no one can work. While I am in the world, I am the light of the world."*
>
> *After saying this, he spit on the ground, made some mud with saliva, and put it on the man's eyes. "Go," he told him, "wash in the Pool of Siloam " (this word means "Sent"). So the man went and washed, and came home seeing.*

Okay, first off, little sidebar: can you imagine that last line of that passage, "He came home seeing." How majestic must have been that walk home for this man? Actually, I bet it wasn't a walk home; I'd bet money that he ran. I mean, for the first time in this guy's life, he gets to see the path in front of him that he was probably used to people helping guide him on every day. But now—he had the ability to run because he could see the ground in front of him. He could see if he was about to run into a tree or a boulder. I bet in the middle of the run, he probably stopped off the path to look at the vibrant colors of the flowers that laid along the side of the road that he never got to see before. I wonder if he looked up at the sky and stood in awe of the clouds and the birds that flew around him. This man woke up not knowing what his bedroom looked like and went home seeing the world that God created around him.

But how much before this miracle this man must have had to suffer. As a child having to learn how to even get around the house safely. I wonder how many nights his parents stayed up anxious and worrying about the dangers that he could get hurt on if he wandered off on his own without the ability to see in front of him. It must have been a learning curve for this man to have to adapt to having a "normal life" like others and just traveling down the road to the marketplace to get groceries. I bet there were days when this man grew frustrated, where the tears flowed down, and he wondered if the suffering would ever end.

But not only did Christ heal him by bringing an end to his suffering, he showed that at the end of the suffering, the glory of God's powers were revealed. Without this man being blind, Jesus wouldn't have been able to show that He did in fact have the power of God in heaven flowing through His veins. Without this man suffering, he wouldn't have been able to experience what it felt like to be healed by the One who created him. So, I think I'm learning from these verses, and in the case of our accident, that sometimes suffering will be long. I guess that's why it's called "long-suffering." And although we may come across a horrific situation to have to endure and suffer through without an end date in sight, that doesn't always mean that it's caused by our sins. Sometimes we will have to endure consequences by others not following Christ, and the result may hurt us because of it. But I want to encourage you that even though we are told we're going to go through challenging times, and while that may anger us that God would allow that to happen, we can know for certain that He allows these trials out of love.

God is the same way that a parent doesn't just throw their child into the deep end of the pool and abandon them when they are trying to learn how to swim; instead, the parent gets in the shallow end with the child. There may be moments where they let go of the child so they can learn to feel the water and experience the fear of panic because that drives them to learn to hold themselves up. They aren't far away though; the parent is ready to grab the child before they go all the way under. And in the same way, Christ may allow us to go through some panic and difficult times in order to prepare us for deeper waters later on. Him allowing us to suffer trials before the biggest challenges that will come later is part of the most loving thing that He can do. He doesn't abandon us; He is just teaching us how to swim.

Here are some helpful quotes I've read that have helped encourage me along this train of thought on the road of long-suffering:

*"God has not been trying an experiment on my faith or love in order to find out their quality. He knew it already. It was I who didn't. In this trial, he makes me occupy the dock, the witness box, and the jury bench all at once. He always knew that my temple was a house of cards. His only way for making me realize the fact was to knock it down."*[2] *– C.S. Lewis*

"Why, then, did God give them free will? Because free will though it makes evil possible, is also the only thing that makes possible any love or goodness or joy worth having."[3] - C.S. Lewis; Mere Christianity

"Jesus never promised to eliminate all of the chaos from our lives; He said He'd bring meaning to it."[4] - Bob Goff

"There is a reason the sky gets dark at night. We were not to see everything all the time. We were meant to rest and trust even in darkness."[5] - Morgan Harper Nichols

"You will see light one day. And it will be so beautiful, so bright, that it will be worth waiting all of those months in the dark for."[6] - (Anonymous)

I'm pretty new to running. In fact, I have a difficult time even calling myself a "runner" because I don't feel like I have the experience or that I'm fast enough to have the right to use that title. I've only been running for a few years, and in that time, I wasn't even physically able to run with my injuries. While I've had good days on being able to set new, personal records with mile times or distance in my short time of running, I still have a lot of shortcomings that I struggle with in this sport.

One of my biggest hurdles is pace. I have absolutely no idea how to set a pace and continue in that groove for the remainder of the run. I get in my own head, often running as fast as I can my first mile, trying to beat my previous mile time records, and then by mile two, I'm often exhausted and have a hard time even just moving my legs. I used to be able to get by on this, to run miles on miles each day even if I was winded because my body was strong and fit. But now—I'm still learning to move in this new literally wired body. I haven't been able to get up to more than a 5K running distance since our accident where, before, I went all the way to completing a 50K.

A few months ago, just a month after I was cleared by my spinal doctor to have permission to run again, my dad and I signed up for a 5K run on the beach on Coronado Island in San Diego. For the weeks leading up to it, I was struggling hardcore during training. I wasn't able to make it more than the two-mile mark without walking. But I was determined that on that race day with my dad, I was going to run the entire 3.1 miles without any walking breaks.

As we got to the beach that day, surrounded by the hundreds of other runners competing beside us, we stretched our legs and got our distance trackers set on our phones. And before they sounded the alarm to begin the race, my dad told me something that became the only reason I was able to run that entire race that day—he told me to pace myself. He told me to prepare myself and not get caught up in the Adrenaline of the race and the people around me where I would start off the race as quick as I could. He reminded me that in order to complete the race, and be able to run the whole distance, I had to pace myself and not run my hardest so that I could have energy to get to the finish line.

When he first told me this, admittedly I didn't think it was going to be a problem. I wasn't sure why he was telling me that I needed to be concerned about this because I couldn't run that fast anyway. But then they had us line up at the starting line, and as soon as the horn sounded, I understood what my dad meant. I saw others around me taking off and running quickly, and I felt in my mind that I didn't want to be left behind.

A big problem I always face when I run is my breathing. Even before my injuries, and when I was at my peak running days of running 5Ks or 10Ks daily, heck, even when I was running my 50K, I remember moments of struggling to breath. I don't know how to have a breathing pattern or how to take the right number of breaths with each step. So nearly every time I go out for a run, I go into a slight panic attack when I'm struggling to breath.

But on that race day with my dad, I noticed that this wasn't as big of an issue as before. Usually when I'm running by myself, I'm constantly battling my mind and trying to calm myself when I want to catch my breath and, at the same time, pushing my legs to go faster to beat my time. And every time I'd run and go into this panicking fear, I'd not only get scared because I was winded but because of the fact of being alone by myself. And because my pace isn't consistent, I lose my breath rather quickly. But not on that beach with my dad by my side.

Instead, I listened to him. And for the first time in my years of running, I hardly had any issues with my breathing, nor a panic attack. God was teaching me that day in the middle of that race that this is my attitude a lot of times in my everyday life as well. I try to run ahead and keep the pace with everyone else around me. I try to run ahead because I see the next checkpoint or accomplishment, and I think I can get there quicker by doing it at my own pace.

But ya know what happens when I run faster than I'm supposed to? I go ahead of the Father and things start getting difficult. I get worn down, and go into a panic, because He's not alongside me anymore. In the same way that my dad told me to pace myself, so does Christ tell us as He guides us through our lives. He tells us to pace ourselves with Him because He knows our limits more than we do. At the same time, He does allow us to have free will. But the minute we run ahead, He's no longer in our faces—we aren't abiding in Him.

So just like that day when I paced myself with my dad, it wasn't pain-free. It was tough work and I struggled with pain in my back and nervousness with not being able to complete the race without walking. But I trusted my dad; I followed his pace and stayed by his side so that I could have the strength and endurance to keep going.

*"Life isn't a sprint, it's a marathon."*[7] *- (Anonymous)*

And the only way to finish the race glorifying Christ is to go at His pace. Being patient in the waiting is hard. But our abiding in His pace shows our surrender and trust in Him with our lives. Crossing the finish line is only doable by abiding in and with Him.

*"Everyone who goes on ahead and does not abide in the teaching of Christ, does not have God. Whoever abides in the teaching has both the Father and the Son."* 2 John 1:9

*"God is a God of redemption. But He never promised to redeem situations according to our expectations."* ~Jordan Dooley; soulscripts

As Devin and I were out driving a few months back, we started talking about the crash, and the conversation went to this question, "If you could ask for a miracle, what would it be?" We thought about it for a few minutes and threw out a few ideas for different circumstances in life. I think a lot of people in the world would probably ask for world peace, for God to heal cancer and other deadly diseases the world is suffering from. But we started zeroing in on our own personal lives.

I mentioned to Devin how a similar topic had come up in my mind when my mom was sick and in her last few weeks of life from her battle of cancer. I remember in that time I watched her becoming frailer as the cancer was eating away at her, as she grew weaker and unable to eat and even walk on her own. My prayers were no longer asking God to just heal her. But they turned into that if the things she was facing and that our family was having to endure as we began saying goodbyes to our mom, wife, and grandma, this was no longer asking God for a miracle to heal her. But prayers turned into asking Christ to not let her suffer anymore and to free her of pain quickly, even if those words meant that she would no longer get to walk this earth beside us.

And now being on the other side of that chapter of losing Mom, and it being three years later without getting to experience her presence anymore, I think about the fact that I don't think I would ask God for a miracle right now. Sure, I know He could have at any point healed her earthly body and given her many more years of life in this world with us. But that season of heartbreak and suffering actually grew my faith so much deeper, and my love for my mom so much stronger.

Because of that season, my mom and I were able to reconcile years of previous hurt and heartbreak, and the love that God allowed me to feel in my heart for my mom in her final days was something that I had never been able to experience before. My entire life before that I walked in fear of my mom, and I was constantly afraid of the ways that she could hurt me. Yes, I loved her because Christ told me too, but admittedly I struggled with actually loving her, and I know that without my faith in Christ, I wouldn't have been able to.

But during that heartbreaking season, my faith was stretched. What I knew of love before was out the window, and God taught me what true, unconditional love meant. I was able to hold the hand of someone who once hurt me with those same hands and be able to pour out all my love on her. With the same mouth that used to yell words of painful words my way, I was now hearing "I love you" from. And the woman who used to scare me more than anyone, I now pitied and cried over the body that was withering day by day from this terrible disease.

That season of losing Mom grew my faith deeper and in new ways I had never experienced before. There were still moments of yelling happening: there was chaos, and confusion, and hurtful words that were being spoken in the middle of my care taking of Mom. But God used those times to deepen my leaning on Him. There were so many times where I would have to step out of the room with tears pouring down my face as I sat in hurt, but also held so much love in my heart for the person hurting me.

*"Loving each other is what we were meant to do and how we were made to roll. It's not where we start when we begin following Jesus; it's the beautiful path we travel the rest of our lives. Will it be messy and ambiguous and uncomfortable when we love people the way Jesus said to love them? You bet it will. Will we be misunderstood? Constantly. But extravagant love often means coloring outside the lines and going beyond the norms ... Jesus never said these things would be easy. He just said it would work."* [8] - Bob Goff; *Everybody Always*

So no, the miracle I asked for wouldn't be healing my mom from her cancer. Without that terrible season, she and I would not have gotten to experience the healing we did, and I don't know that I ever would have understood what God meant by agape love than in those moments of absolute hell and heartbreak.

But now I'll begin wrapping up this chapter section with this thought. You might be thinking, *So, Jo, would you ask for a miracle with the situation of your car accident?* This is also something I've gone over and over in my mind. And I've come to the conclusion again that no, I actually wouldn't. And as I write those words, it's not an easy conclusion to come to. It really hurts and breaks my heart.

I think about the man that hit us who passed away. I think about Devin's left leg that was shattered and nearly lost in the crash. I think about the bones in my body that were torn apart in the impact. And I think of the life of Enya who was taken so suddenly, and the life she was robbed off because of a careless mistake. As much as I miss her, and as dearly as I love her, I know that this is all a part of God's perfect plan He has written out for our lives.

He allowed these circumstances to happen, and I don't want to run ahead to avoid the pains in order to try to attain something that looks better in my own strength. I don't want to squirm out of these trials and long-sufferings He has allowed us to walk through in order to grow and stretch our faith in Him even more. Without this accident, we wouldn't have been able to reach the people that we did.

I wouldn't have gotten to speak to the nurses in the hospital room about my Bible, Christ, and church. Devin wouldn't have been able to share his deep love he has for me to the doctors and surgeons around him and be a witness of the love Christ has put in his heart. Like the man in the Bible who was born blind, without these injuries and our bodies being torn apart, we wouldn't have been able to experience the healing power of Christ running through our veins and through our bones. I wouldn't have been able to share the love of Jesus to my elderly neighbor in rehab through sharing color pencils and cookies because I wouldn't have had any reason to be in her life otherwise. We wouldn't have been able to show examples of what it means to forgive someone who flipped our lives upside down and took things away from us that we will never get back.

So no, I don't wish for a miracle. There are days, well actually every day, I wish Enya were here with us. I wish we weren't experiencing the aches and shooting pains throughout our healing bodies as they suffer through recovery. And I wish that life looked a bit different, and more like the plan that I had in mind before our crash. But I don't wish that the crash didn't happen anymore when I think deeply about it. Because even though a lot of days it just seems like the pain is unending, I can know for certain that it is a tool God is using through this long-suffering to grow us to look more like Him. This can be an example to show His healing, His power, and His love to those around us by the way we respond to this tragedy happening to us.

# Chapter 14: Forgiveness, Things Left Unsettled, But a Life Left to Live

*"Telling your story is the act of recalling all of the things you've learned from traveling, and then, figuring out how to share those lessons with someone else who is about to take that same trip."*[1] *- Morgan Harper Nichols*

SO HERE WE ARE—OVER a year after the crash. A year of learning to hand over the pieces of this shattered and broken life to a God who has taught us new lessons in each of those broken bits along the way. We're one year in, and life is still unsettled. We haven't had some miraculous improvement in our injuries. But by Christ's mercy and power, we have healed little by little each day and have learned new ways to strengthen these once shattered bodies. We haven't gotten all the pieces of our lives put back into place; in fact, if you have noticed anything along the journey through the chapters of this book, you'll know that life continues to get messy, and right now there are more questions than answers in our lives.

We have faced over 365 days of justice not being served; the life of a man we had never met was lost just moments after impact with us. And the man who was racing him has continued to run and hide instead of coming forward and beginning to show remorse for the damages and the decisions he made that changed and affected the lives of many that night. People often wonder and ask if we have forgiven the men who raced and caused so much grievance in our lives. The answer is yes. We've forgiven them, but we still walk through each day with the reminder of that night by the physical pains in our bodies, and the hole we will always have in our hearts for our girl Enya. We won't get justice for her, because unfortunately the life of our pup being lost is not considered an official crime to be charged with. This is the hardest part of moving forward.

We have wandered through this desert of unanswered questions and upcoming court dates for this past year. We continue to grow in questions, hurts, and just wanting to wrap this part of the story up so that we can move on. Medical bills are a constant fear. We've been hurt by the lack of insurance the men who were racing had, and the alternative and hopes are that our insurance will cover our bills so that we won't owe anything. We never realized that doing absolutely nothing wrong could turn into a worse-case scenario. These men literally committed crimes, and we are left wounded and in a sea of unknowns as a result. It's frustrating and far from over.

Along the pages of this book, I've shared some of my deepest fears, hurts, and the battles that have ripped apart my heart and mind. My hopes are that this never came across as a sob story, but I hope and pray more than anything that this can help someone else who might be on a similar journey up a difficult mountain. This has stretched me to my core, and there have been moments where the words typed out are only because I felt the tug of God pushing me to share this story as a way to be vulnerable, to show the perfectness of God through this imperfect person that I am.

I think there were moments where I felt that this story didn't really matter—that no one would really care to flip the pages and carry on through this story and the lessons I've typed out. Maybe they don't really matter. Maybe no one will ever be affected by these words, or this whole thing could be a flop. But I don't think that's why God was asking me for my obedience in writing this. Maybe He was simply just asking me to show up and allow that to be enough for right now.

I think of it like someone showing up to work for example. Sure, you could skip out on your job tomorrow. Maybe you wouldn't get fired. Maybe your company, whether it's a business association, fast-food joint, or public school system, maybe it wouldn't matter one bit if you showed up or not tomorrow. The whole system could go on and never be affected. But maybe you missed out on a day where God could have placed an opportunity for a conversation with your coworker about the love of Christ for the first time. Maybe you could have noticed something going on inside the mind of a student that other teachers and educators overlooked in their business. Maybe someone made a dig at your boss under their breath in that business meeting and you could've stood up for them.

I don't know what could have happened. But even when the whole system doesn't fall apart because of one decision, sometimes God is still asking us to show up for a specific reason, no matter how small that reason might be. And that's how I feel with this book. It's scary. There's a lot of eyes that could stumble upon these pages and criticize and hurt me as a result of sharing my heart. That's terrifying.

And there's been a nagging voice coming from the enemy lines that has been telling me these words and this story are useless—that no one will ever see these words. Maybe so. But that doesn't stop me from writing them, because I think that maybe God is going to use them, even if it's just in the life of one single person.

We've gone through a wide variety of topics throughout these chapters, from the side effects of medications to what it's like to be on the table in the middle of the emergency room surrounded by trauma doctors. From the ways God has shown up, when maybe others haven't, and then the journey of walking through and navigating through the valley of grief in the middle of it all. These are all topics I never knew could be related to a car crash. But somehow, they've been the mountains we've climbed through this year, and Christ has continually taught us something new on each of those trails along the way.

*****

Musician Keith Green has this great quote I came across recently:

*"If someone writes a great story, people praise the author, not the pen. People don't say, 'Oh what an incredible pen … where can I get a pen like this so I can write great stories?'*

*Well, I'm just a pen in the hands of the Lord. He is the author. All praise should go to Him."* [2]

I love this. I've always struggled with the idea of complementing a pastor on a great sermon, or an author of a Christian book that God spoke through, or a musician who sang the words that explained the love of Christ. I never have understood how someone can praise those people they are the instruments, but God is the one who is behind each of those gifts. And if there is anything that has spoken to you through the pages of this book, I want you to know that it was Christ and never me.

There were so many times where I'd lift my hands from the keyboard and go something like "WOAH, that's so cool!" after typing out something in these chapters. I'd often look over at Devin and explain to him how the words that were just typed were this concept I never had in mind to write, and it was obviously the Holy Spirit working through the tips of my fingers on this keyboard, because I was learning through Him speaking throughout this writing journey.

Christ has allowed me to play this small part in His even bigger story, and I hope that the moments I share in the raw moments have never come across as a victim, but instead as someone who is trying her best to walk in vulnerability. I want you to know that yes, I love Jesus and despite the circumstances we have walked through, I've never doubted He existed or that He loved me. But I want to be real in the way that I have still struggled as a Christ follower with mental health, with anger, with pain, and with walking through uncertainty. I've made a lot of gross mistakes along the way and have wondered often if God was rolling His eyes and I was poking His last nerve with the struggles I was battling.

I know what it's like to feel guilt and shame, wondering if I'm out of God's reach or if I did something wrong that caused the circumstances around me to fall apart. I'm a broken person, living in a broken world, and the only way that I've managed to make it this far is by handing things over to Christ and giving up on trying to sort things out myself. Because whenever I try to get things back together, I seem to make it messier than if I were to just surrender it all to Him to begin with.

*****

*"Sometimes, we need to forgive God. Not because God made a mistake and needs our forgiveness. We need to forgive God because somewhere along the way, God didn't show up, and we've been shutting down our hearts and our willingness to hear and see the work God is doing and the ways God is moving."*[3] *- Caleb Campbell*

I've messed up along this road of life with trying to create and accomplish things on my own timetable, and time and time again, Jesus has tapped me on the shoulder, had me look Him in the eyes, and ask me to hand over my blueprint so that He could take over. Sometimes I've handed them over easily, while other times I have a tight grip and try to sneak one more peak in while reluctantly dropping it in His hands. I've lived through disappointments when I wanted something to go one way, and He allowed doors to be closed and things to fall apart right before my eyes.

I've battled the thoughts on why it's necessary for me to undergo all these hard things, and why He can let up on a life for a sec for me to catch my breath. I understand what it's like to be disappointed in the life He has given us instead of being grateful for the life He has allowed me to have, even when it didn't measure up to the expectations or plan I had in mind. That doesn't mean He didn't show up. And He definitely didn't give up on me. He simply allowed certain things to happen and life to get messy sometimes in order for me to learn what it means to lean on Him, to strengthen my faith in ways I didn't know I needed but He knew I did along the way.

*****

*"You thought all along that it would be your mastery that would take you into new places in life. But it's not. Turns out, it's your vulnerability."*
⁴ - Leeana Tankersley

Growing up, my parents used to talk about how the softball field was my mission field. They'd often tell the stories of the times when I was little just starting off on the field; when making new friends, I would always ask a series of questions:

-What's your name?

-How many teeth have you lost?

-Do you believe in Jesus?

I have lots of memories of inviting teammates to church with me, or summer camps and them getting to grow to know Christ through those camp days, while some other not-so-great memories, like the time I sat on the bench while awaiting my turn at bat and turned to my fellow teammate who I learned had never heard of God before. Astonished, I quickly grew concerned for her from everything that I had learned in my whole seven years of life and the topic of God, Satan, and heaven and hell. I immediately explained that she had to get to know Jesus because otherwise she would go to hell when she died one day. Whoops ... yeah, that wasn't one of my best moments on the "mission field."

And while I've learned to handle that topic a little more gracefully, and a lot more lovingly, my heart hasn't really strayed from its initial concern. I want people to know Jesus, not because I don't want them to suffer in hell but because I want them to know and experience the love that He gives us in this life, and the hope He gives us before eternity as well.

So, I think it's kind of ironic that the whole backstory of this book has taken place because of an accident just a few hundred feet away from that softball field where I played in a softball game, just minutes before our crash. And somehow the mission field didn't stay on the field that night, and it worked through the street near the field where our car was crashed into. Where our story of the life He allowed us to continue to live and share with others has gone on. Where God has shown a miracle through the protection He gave us that night and used it to point to His glory through it all.

*****

*"I cling onto your memory, not to wallow in the darkness, but to remember the light that you brought into my world."*[5] *- Mark Lemon*

A big part of this book I wanted to share is my heart and the legacy that Enya has left behind in my life, as well as so many people she encountered in her short time on earth. While I'll never go a day without missing her presence beside me or getting to see her smiling face first thing in the morning, I've learned how to be thankful for the lessons she taught me along the way, even when grieving the loss of her life. God taught me more lessons that I can count through the love and the life Enya lived each day through defiant joy, doing things afraid, and loving unconditionally.

I'm learning that it's okay to feel the heartbreak of never getting to hold my sweet pup again, while missing her bark, running with her through the park, driving her to get ice cream, and getting to bury my face in her furry chest on a hard day: and while feeling all of these things, I can also simultaneously remember the moments of joy that we did get to share in with her, and be comforted by those joy-filled memories as we travel through life with the grief of her in our hearts.

Earlier today, I went for a run with my friend Katie. Along the path of our run, there was a rock garden overlooking a beautiful section of one of our local beaches. She came up with the idea recently to paint some rocks for someone she lost and loved and invited me to also color a rock for Enya as well. Today we sat and ate breakfast after our run, and then colored our rocks for the ones that we loved and lost along the way. We shared stories and memories of special moments we got to live through with them and the things we missed about them no longer being by our sides anymore.

With tears coming down my face, but trying to hide behind my sunglasses, I shared how it's a difficult thing to walk through knowing that I did everything I could to make a safe environment for Enya in our car every car ride. When she wasn't sticking her head out the window while I held tightly to her harness, she would always sprawl out across my lap, where I'd always wrap my arms around her and hold her closely.

But I never imagined that it would be the position that we would be in during the impact of our crash, where I thought she would be safe and protected but I was wrong. My arms didn't protect her head from a concussion, or from her back from breaking like mine but worse. I shared with my friend how it's both a debt I can never repay Enya for, but also a heavy load to carry knowing that she shielded me from the brunt of the impact that night. She sacrificed everything for me. This is what everyone said, and something I'm both thankful for and hate all at once.

When I was finished sharing this, Katie shared words with me that touched my heart and helped lighten the load I was carrying over this topic. She said, "Without Enya's protection, my friend wouldn't be here with me today." While this is touching and also heartbreaking, it reminds me to keep going not only in thankfulness that I got the opportunity to live, but also to not take for granted the life that Enya allowed me to have because of her protection. I know God used her as my angel pup to protect me that night.

*****

*"Friendly reminder: when I'm resting because my body isn't functioning properly, I need to remember that I'm not wasting my day staying in bed. I'm recovering. Which is exactly what my body needs."*[6] *- (Anonymous)*

I fought the idea of writing this book for a long time. I think God put in my heart nearly ten years ago this passion for writing to point others to Him. For many years, I struggled with the idea of wanting to write a book, but also not feeling like I had a big enough story to tell that would stretch on for more than a few pages, or even impact people around me. But it's funny how after years of struggling, I suddenly had this story fall in my lap. After a lot of cruddy and unfortunate circumstances; through those terrible moments, He kept giving me new lessons and words to share with others along the way.

I had a hard time getting started this year with writing all of these thoughts and ideas down. I knew how much they meant to me as they were given to me from God. But every time I got started, I'd talk myself out of it. I believed others just wouldn't care. I struggled physically and mentally with having the energy to even get out of bed some days. I beat myself up over the lack of work I've been able to accomplish this past year with all my injuries. There have been so many days where I physically couldn't get out of bed. I felt like I was falling behind, like my peers were judging me for not keeping up with them or making a difference in this world.

And while I haven't been able to work full time, it was like God was handing me my keyboard over and telling me, "Hey, ya know you can type those ideas out while also lying in bed in pain." And He was right. I've typed out the majority of these words from the embrace of our comforter in our bed, while I often was nursing a migraine, spinal spasms, or a collarbone (or lack thereof) throbbing.

He's taught me that there were days to push through and continue to type out this story, and other days where I couldn't lift my hands; and on those days, it wasn't part of His plans for me to write. On those days, He wasn't teaching me to be strong and persevere. No, He was teaching me another lesson rest, and the importance of not feeling like the world depends on my productivity in order to go around. On those days, rest is what my body needs. So while I'm still struggling with feeling like enough, or wondering what others think about me because I don't work full time, I'm also really grateful for this opportunity Christ has allowed, and the words He has given me through this passion I have for writing.

I don't know the rest of our story yet, and I know I'm going to continue to mess up and struggle throughout my future days with wanting the hard things to end, and, at the same time, knowing my God is holding us through it all. This year has felt really yucky at times, and there are a lot of lessons I wish we didn't have to learn but still were necessary for our faith. It felt really difficult at times, and most weeks it still does. Devin put it this way, which I feel like sums it up pretty perfectly:

*"It's more like when you go in for a close shave, but instead of a barber, it's a runaway car. And instead of a knife, it's a 100 mph collision. And instead of cutting just a tad bit too much hair off, it's a deep tear of your leg while you bleed out on the side of the street, praying your wife's not dead and you're not about to die."*

So, we don't know how everything is going to play out through the endless desert of court, whether or not Devin or myself will ever need another surgery again on one of the places in our bodies that was injured during the crash. We don't know if we'll ever do certain sports again, whether we'll encounter more unknowns or more questions along the way. But there is something we do know. That night, the moment that car lost control and made impact with our Mini Cooper at 100 miles per hour—that should have been it. No one understood how and why we lived to see another day. But we know why; Christ has something more in store for us. Maybe it's just one more day of helping someone in their journey. Maybe it's to share in one more conversation with someone we love. Or maybe to share Jesus with someone who has never heard His name before. Our lives could go one more hour, or eighty more years. And regardless of how long it is, we know that each second, each moment is a part of the life He saved us for.

*"And they lived modestly ever after." ~Devin Quarles*

# Bibliography

Introduction

1. TerKeurst, L [@LysaTerKeurst] (2019, April, 3) "Scars are beautiful when we see them as glorious reminders that we courageously survived... when we let them tell the story of our God who fights for us, heals us, and faithfully sees us through." [Tweet] Twitter. https://twitter.com/lysaterkeurst/status/1113517289272483846

2. *Sorkin, A . (2017). Molly's Game [Film]. STXfilmsH. BrothersTMP .The MG Company.*

Chapter 1: At The Scene

1. *"Our life on earth is a testing ground on what kind of servant we are in heaven." (Anonymous)*

2. *Narrative Citation: According to Beth Moore "God will not make your life manageable; otherwise, you would manage it."*

3. *Gillham, P. (2002). Grace in Ungracious Places. Fleming H Revell Co.*

4. *Albom, M. (2021). Stranger in the lifeboat. Harper.*

Chapter 2: Demanding The Plan

1. *Olson, K. (2022). For the One Trying To Make Sense of the Struggle.* https://proverbs31.org/read/devotions/full-post/2022/03/11/for-the-one-trying-to-make-sense-of-the-struggle

2. *Oxford University Press. (n.d.) Secure. Oxford English dictionary. Retrieved September 25, 2022, from* https://www.oed.com/view/Entry/258346?redirectedFrom=secure

Chapter 3: Enya & God's Mercy
1. C.S. Lewis. (1961). *A grief observed*. HarperOne.
2. Josh Billings. https://www.goodreads.com/quotes/13267-a-dog-is-the-only-thing-on-earth-that-loves
3. Elizabeth Elliot. https://www.goodreads.com/quotes/1051525-sometimes-fear-does-not-subside-and-one-must-choose-to-do-it
4. Jeffers, S. (2006) *Feel the Fear and Do It Anyway*. Ballantine Books
5. Ehman, K. (2022) *Learning To Live in a World With Unanswered "Whys"*. Proverbs 31 Ministries
6. Terkeurst Lysa. (2018) *It's Not Supposed To Be This Way*. Thomas Nelson.
7. Chloe Frayne. https://www.all-greatquotes.com/i-will-love-you-for-the-rest-of-my-life/

Chapter 4: Distance Between Hospital Rooms
1. Terkeurst Lysa. (2018) *It's Not Supposed To Be This Way*. Thomas Nelson.
2. Jennae Cecelia. [instagram] https://www.instagram.com/jennaececelia/?hl=en
3. "If you find that your mind wanders while you're praying, maybe you should pray about what your mind keeps wandering to."(Anonymous)
4. Vanauken S. (2009) *A Severe Mercy*. HarperOne
5. A.W. Tozer https://www.goodreads.com/quotes/1346489-when-i-understand-that-everything-happening-to-me-is-to

Chapter 5: Final ICU Days, Rehabilitation & Hopelessness
1. Eugene Paterson. https://www.goodreads.com/quotes/216967-when-we-submit-our-lives-to-what-we-read-in
2. Stroble L. (2014) *Case for Faith*. Zondervan

3. *"If someone says you can't do it; do it twice and take pictures."* (Anonymous) https://quotecollectorsclub.com/when-someone-says-you-cant-do-it/
4. J.K. Rowling (2009) *Harry Potter and the Deathly Hallows.* Arthur A. Levine Books

Chapter 6: Recovery At Home

1. @motherwwortandrose *"What if broken dreams are not a waste, but compost?"*
2. Shirer P. (2015) *The Armor of God.* Lifeway Press
3. *"Go laugh in the places that you've cried. Change the narrative."* (Anonymous) https://loveexpands.com/go-laugh-in-the-places-you-have-cried-change-the-narrative/
4. Lusko L. (2022) *The Last Supper on the moon.* Thomas Nelson

Chapter 7: Medications & Mental Health

1. @disabilityhealth *"You are not your intrusive thoughts. They're kind of like weeds. Yeah, they're in the garden, but you sure as heck didn't plant them."* [Tumbler] https://www.tumblr.com/misha-kastrilevich/179417607927/teaforyourginaa-disabilityhealth-you-are-not
2. EMDR Institute, Inc. (2020) https://www.emdr.com/what-is-emdr/
3. Stoecklein K. (2020) *Fear Gone Wild.* Thomas Nelson

Chapter 8: Sitting Still

1. Elliot E. (2004) *Secure in the Everlasting Arms.* Revell
2. Goff, B [@bobgoff] (2022, September 3) *"I keep putting things in the microwave, and God keeps putting them back in the crockpot. Whatever is distracting you today, give it a little more time."* [Tweet] Twitter. https://twitter.com/bobgoff/status/1566099896142245888?lang=en

3. Morgan Harper Nichols @morganharpernichols "Perhaps 'keep going' does not have to mean 'keep running.' Perhaps to simply keep breathing is a miraculous feat all on its own ... especially right now." https://www.instagram.com/p/Cah0z8LJX0B/?hl=en

Chapter 9: Loneliness

1. Dr. Glenn Patrick Doyle [@DrDoyleSays] "Some of us might feel more lonely around people than we ever do when we're actually alone." [Tweet] Twitter.
2. Dr. Glenn Patrick Doyle [@DrDoyleSays] (2022, September 17) "No complex trauma survivor's trying to..." [Tweet] Twitter. https://twitter.com/DrDoyleSays/status/1571242589948444672

Chapter 10: Some Tough Questions

1. Foster M. "Within the valleys of our grief, something beautiful wants to grow. Tend those fields, water those little seeds. What was planted in pain, can harvest beautiful possibilities."
2. "Grief is like surfing. Except you're blindfolded. In a hurricane. And your surfboard is on fire. And the people on the shore are shouting surfing strategies for a storm they've never surfed and then shaking their heads at how you handle the waves." (Anonymous)
3. Ribble K. (2021) Love me in the Waiting. Dexterity
4. Billy Graham "My home is in heaven. I'm just traveling through this world."

Chapter 11: Fear of Flying

1. Craig Groeshel. @craiggroeschel https://www.instagram.com/p/B5-jzsyjeRE/?hl=en
2. Aaron Paul Sullivan [@apsullivan] (2021, October 28) "Having anxiety is like being in an argument with an idiot..." [Tweet] Twitter. https://twitter.com/apsullivan/status/1453900501817384983

3. Dion K. "They say 'one day at a time,' but there have been an awful lot of one hour at a time's in those days and one minute at a time's in those hours. Whatever 'one' you are working on right now, I'm proud of you." https://americasbestpics.com/picture/they-say-one-day-at-a-time-but-there-have-9rwe8oKS8

4. "When God says 'don't' we should read that as 'Don't hurt yourself.'" (Anonymous)

5. Dad Jokes. [@Dadsaysjokes] (2021, April 19) "Who's the genius that decided to call it "Emotional baggage "...and not "griefcase." [Tweet] Twitter https://twitter.com/dadsaysjokes/status/1384271449389637637

Chapter 12: Body Image

1. Elisabeth Elliot "Waiting on God requires the willingness to bear uncertainty—to carry within oneself the unanswered question, lifting the heart to God about it whenever it intrudes upon one's thoughts." https://www.goodreads.com/quotes/360360-i-do-know-that-waiting-on-god-requires-the-willingness

2. Mayo Clinic. Mayo Foundation for Medical Education and Research. https://www.mayoclinic.org/diseases-conditions/body-dysmorphic-disorder/symptoms-causes/syc-20353938?utm_source=Google&utm_medium=abstract&utm_content=Body-dysmorphic-disorder&utm_campaign=Knowledge-panel

3. "If you can't yet say kind things about your body then maybe focus on not saying mean things to your body first." (Anonymous)

4. Gail Dines "If tomorrow, women woke up and decided they really liked their bodies, imagine how many industries would go out of business." https://www.goodreads.com/quotes/7039716-if-tomorrow-women-woke-up-and-decided-they-really-liked

5. Ross Edgley. *"This body is an instrument to use, not an ornament to be displayed."*

6. Dr. Glenn Patrick Doyle [@DrDoyleSays] (2022, March 25) *"Nobody recovers from trauma while hating and punishing themselves. Nobody blames and shames themselves into a better headspace."* [Tweet] Twitter. https://twitter.com/drdoylesays/status/1507352098593132548

7. J.A. Medders *"We often think Christian maturity is needing help less and less. Wrong. Maturity is realizing how dependent we are on Jesus more and more. Self-reliance is self-sabotage."* https://m.facebook.com/1742489815978618/photos/we-often-think-christian-maturity-is-needing-help-less-and-less-wrong-maturity-i/2581032288791029/

8. *"A Jesus who never wept could never wipe away my tears."* -Charles H. Spurgeon

9. Charles Spurgeon *"Consider how precious a soul must be, when both God and the devil are after it."* https://www.goodreads.com/quotes/221612-a-jesus-who-never-wept-could-never-wipe-away-my

10. *"Eating enough food: You must eat enough food to recover. It will also help to eliminate urges to binge. And normalize cravings for your fear foods. If you're restricting, you will be malnourished and not be in the best mental state to tackle fears. The key to being able to normalize and neutralize fear foods is eating enough food to restore your body and mind."* (Anonymous)

11. *"Photos are only 'snapshots' of particular moments, angles, and doesn't mean they always accurately depict the object. For instance, we may take a photo of a beautiful scenery and then say. 'Well, the photo doesn't capture the actual beauty of the scenery,' but we don't*

say, 'It's not that beautiful in the photo, therefore the scenery must actually not be that amazing.'" (Anonymous)

12. Joshua Fletcher [@anxietyjosh] "There are chemicals in my body and false signals in my brain making me feel this way—this is not me. Tolerating this is strength, not weakness. What I decided to do next is important." [Tweet] Twitter

13. "Do you suppose that the same Son of God that stood in the furnace with Shadrach, Meshach, and Abednego is not also standing with you? Your furnace may look different than theirs but the One alongside you has not changed." (Anonymous)

14. Liberty Underwood. (2019) *Little Heart, Rest Here.*

15. Charles Spurgeon "He who counts the stars and calls them by their names is in no danger of forgetting His own children."

16. Christine Caine (2019) *Undaunted: Daring to do what God calls you to do.* Thomas Nelson

17. Bree Lenehan [@breeelenehan] "You can't love only the 'socially acceptable' parts of you, without embracing all the things that make you YOU. You can't love your body under the conditions of looking 'perfect' and posed, without also accepting the rolls, lumps and bumps that come along with it. You can't give your time, love, and effort to relationships that only love your 'best' either." [Instagram]

18. "Mosaics are made from broken pieces, but they're still beautiful works of art, and so are you.." (Anonymous) https://www.pinterest.com/pin/573083121306700704/

19. Goff, B [@bobgoff] (2019, January 18) "When people ask me what it looks like to follow Jesus, I say following Him looks like dealing with all of the issues everyone else does disappointments, tremendous joy, uncertainty and having your mind constantly change as

you learn how Jesus would have dealt with these emotions." [Tweet] Twitter https://twitter.com/bobgoff/status/1086315180865277952?lang=en

20. Charles Spurgeon (2020) *Encouragement for the Depressed*. Crossway

## Chapter 13: Is This Never-ending? Or Maybe It's Long-suffering

1. Helen Dunmore (2009) *The Deep*. HarperTeen
2. C.S. Lewis (2015) *A Grief Observed*. HarperOne
3. C.S. Lewis (2015) *Mere Christianity*. HarperOne
4. Goff, B [@bobgoff] (2018 December 19) "Jesus never promised to eliminate all of the chaos from our lives; He said He'd bring meaning to it." [Tweet] Twitter https://twitter.com/bobgoff/status/1075415457694285827?lang=en
5. Morgan Harper Nichols @morganhnichols "There is a reason the sky gets dark at night. We were not to see everything all the time. We were meant to rest and trust even in darkness." [Tweet] Twitter https://twitter.com/morganhnichols/status/986462148669800449?lang=en
6. "You will see light one day. And it will be so beautiful, so bright, that it will be worth waiting all of those months in the dark for." (Anonymous)
7. "Life isn't a sprint, it's a marathon." (Anonymous)
8. Bob Goff. (2018) *Everybody Always*. Nelson Books

## Chapter 14: Forgiveness, Things Left Unsettled, But a Life Left to Live

1. Morgan Harper Nichols @morganharpernichols "Telling your story is the act of recalling all of the things you've learned from traveling, and then, figuring out how to share those lessons with someone else who is about to take that same trip." [Instagram]

2. Keith Green. "Well, I'm just a pen in the hands of the Lord. He is the author. All praise should go to Him." https://www.azquotes.com/author/24221-Keith_Green#:~:text=Well%2C%20I%20am%20just%20a,praise%20should%20go%20to%20him.&text=The%20only%20music%20minister%20to,important%20part%20of%20their%20life.
3. Caleb Campbell "Sometimes, we need to forgive God. Not because God made a mistake and needs our forgiveness. We need to forgive God because somewhere along the way, God didn't show up, and we've been shutting down our hearts and our willingness to hear and see the work God is doing and the ways God is moving."
4. Leeana Tankersley "You thought all along that it would be your mastery that would take you into new places in life. But it's not. Turns out, it's your vulnerability."
5. Mark Lemon "I cling onto your memory, not to wallow in the darkness, but to remember the light that you brought into my world."
6. "Friendly reminder: when I'm resting because my body isn't functioning properly, I need to remember that I'm not wasting my day staying in bed. I'm recovering. Which is exactly what my body needs." (Anonymous)

www.ingramcontent.com/pod-product-compliance
Lightning Source LLC
Chambersburg PA
CBHW020353170426
43200CB00005B/148